A MINORITY GROUP IN AMERICAN SOCIETY

McGRAW-HILL SOCIAL PROBLEMS SERIES

Marvin B. Sussman, Series Editor

The purpose of this series is to provide new and improved materials for teaching the introductory course in social problems. In order to serve the needs of this and related courses the series brings together a set of stimulating and thought-provoking original volumes which deal with the traditional social problem areas. By covering relevant theory and research, each volume becomes a provocative study of ideas and conceptualizations rather than a descriptive account of a particular social problem. Each provides a theoretical framework relative to the problem under study. Together the volumes offer the instructor an opportunity to develop an integrative conceptual framework for the introductory social problems course.

NOW AVAILABLE

J. Milton Yinger • A MINORITY GROUP IN AMERICAN SOCIETY

IN PREPARATION

Leonard Savitz • CRIME AND DELINQUENCY
Harrison Trice • ALCOHOLISM AND DRUG ADDICTION
Joseph W. Eaton • MENTAL HEALTH
Marvin B. Sussman • FAMILY
Robert Dentler • COMMUNITY
Vincent H. Whitney • POPULATION
William A. Fraunce • PROBLEMS OF AN INDUSTRIAL SOCIETY

A MINORITY GROUP
IN AMERICAN SOCIETY

J. MILTON YINGER

Department of Sociology and Anthropology,
Oberlin College

McGRAW-HILL BOOK COMPANY
New York · St. Louis · San Francisco · Toronto · London · Sydney

EDITOR'S INTRODUCTION

The decade of the 1960s will be known as the one which challenged the world, particularly the United States, to solve the critical problem of intergroup relations. Either it will go down in history as a decade in which a tempered citizenry in this country solved the problems of racial, ethnic, and religious injustice or it will be remembered as one in which the seeds of hatred, distrust, and violence burst forth so widely and extravagantly as to destroy in a moment a century of hard-won gains in civil rights and social justice.

The message of *It Can't Happen Here* by Sinclair Lewis is as appropriate to the problems of today as it was to those of the 1930s. When rational men are no longer rational, when religious men become bigots, and when shopkeepers become racists, then the social order will change and extremists of the left or the right will take over.

In a brilliant paper, Kenneth Boulding describes the traps of a postcivilization period, a period which began in 1949 when the USSR mastered the secret of nuclear fission, when international rocketry with thermonuclear warheads became a reality, and the possibility of world destruction increased. Unilateral action on the part of a major power was ruled out and the responsibility presented by this awesome technology required advanced thinking and ways of settling issues as we entered a postcivilization period. War of the pre-1949 period has become virtually obsolete as a major technique for solving international and intergroup conflicts. *War is the principal trap of mankind.*

Unrestrained population growth (the current world "birthquake") and continuous worldwide waste of irreplaceable natural and human resources are two additional traps of mankind.

The first trap, the threat of a thermonuclear war, is of major concern. The 1960s will go down in history as a period of military stalemate and one in which economic and ideological thrusts dominated the struggle for world power and control. The greatest threat of military conflict involving thermonuclear weaponry occurred in 1962 during the Cuban confrontation between the United States and the USSR. Since that time, many theories have been advanced concerning the bases for the resolution of the conflict and the subsequent "warming up" of the cold war. What were the principal factors which led to a withdrawal of Russian rocketry and the eventual movement away from the brink of war? Experts in international affairs have offered many explanations and one cannot be certain which one is correct. A feasible explanation is that Russian leadership has recognized that war is a trap which can destroy Russian society and thereby their hope for a new world order. The USSR has not given up the struggle for ideological and political domination of its avowed enemies or of the uncommitted peoples in the world. Simply, it has decided to stake its future and ultimate success in achieving world domination not upon war but upon what it perceives as the self-destruction propensities of non-Communist nations.

The self-destruction tendencies of non-Communist nations are cyclical economic collapse and consequent large-scale unemployment, and conflict among class, racial, ethnic, and religious groups. These conditions are interrelated. In the classic interpretations of Marxist doctrine concerned with the ultimate defeat of capitalistic nations by "superior" socialist states, one recurrent theme is that the world economy of capitalism cannot possibly expand or grow each year, a condition requisite to the survival of capitalism. Moreover, economic depressions will occur with increasing severity, each depression worse than the one preceding, and the ultimate outcome is the collapse of capitalism. It was fully expected that in capitalistic countries in the postwar period, the 1929–1933 depression with its declining economic output and severe crises and conflicts would recur. Only the war, Soviet economists believed, with its full employment and *ersatz* prosperity, saved the American economy from a number of crippling economic depressions.

Contrary to these expectations, the world economy of the capitalist nations has continued to grow, and the prospects for continuous growth over the next ten years without a lengthy depression are predicted. Soviet economists concede that industrial production growth in the United States will expand from a 2–2.5 rate annually to between 2.75 and 3.25 percent.[1] These views underscore those of Eugen Varga, another Soviet economist, who was severely criticized in the late 1940s for his prediction that prosperity and not recession was in store for the Western countries in the postwar period. It is interesting that this growth is attributed more to modernization of the industrial system with its improved technology and research than to an economy based upon armaments. Although armaments play an important role in the economy of a modern society, according to Manukyan, they play a lesser role in the current upward pattern of prosperity than they did a decade ago.

The significance of this new Soviet view on the outlook for world capitalism is that the Communist posture of imminent economic failure

1. Harry Schwartz, "Russian Economist Reverses the Usual View of Capitalism," *New York Times,* September 6, 1964, pp. 1, 11. Report of Mr. Schwartz on an article by Mr. A. Manukyan in *Mirovaya Ekonomika i Mezhdunarodnyye Otnosheniya.*

for capitalist nations is "old hat." War is no longer a satisfactory method to defeat capitalism. If economic collapse is not likely, what then?

Logically, one of the Soviet's remaining cards to play is a social revolution spawned in the hate and fury of conflict of minority groups in a highly differentiated and stratified American society. The social problem of minority group relations is our society's most pressing problem today. Its lack of resolution germinates the seeds of destruction of a free democratic society and prepares the ideological foundation for seizure of power within and for supportive action by the Communist world without.

The problems of intergroup relations in American society are directly related to the East-West ideological struggle for the allegiance of the 1 billion uncommitted peoples of Africa, Asia, and Melanesia. One prerequisite for the survival and continuity of a society is its ability to sustain its own societal system. To accomplish this, the consent of other societies is required, or the consequence is war and possible annihilation of one's system. In a world so divided in ideological conflict, universal consent is impossible. At best one can achieve a balance of power with international bodies such as the United Nations functioning to arbitrate disputes. However, it is still necessary to gather to one's side friendly allies and to keep uncommitted those nations which refuse to assume a stance. In a figurative sense, commitments are being made daily, and the audience is watching the actors on the world stage playing to the theme of intergroup relations. The simple question is—How does this nation, which has attained the highest standard of living for the largest number of people in the history of mankind, handle the problems of its minority groups and abolish the barriers against individuals' achieving the *largesse* of that society because of membership in a particular cultural or racial group? The world watches, waits, and will decide. On this decision rides the ultimate resolution of the question of whether our society can maintain over time its system of action in consonance with its value system.

It is for these reasons that the minority problem is the majority problem today, begging for understanding, analysis, and solution. In this short volume, Professor Yinger presents a systematic analysis of the status of minority group relations in the United States and suggests a number of strategies which may effect further integration of minorities into the mainstream of American life.

The conceptual framework used by Professor Yinger in this book is one of structure-function. More precisely, it is functional analysis: That which occurs is essentially the outcome of a particular type of structure. The basic element of structure is role, and role relationships characterize the system of the structure. Societies are organized around a set of goals, and roles are performed in relation to these goals. Conflicts arise over disagreements on means to ends, when goals are not commonly shared by members of the society. Learning one's roles and the norms and rules appropriate to these roles is requisite to the maintenance of the structure. Role learning is the major task of the socialization process and is guided by the system of values shared by the society. It is apparent, as Professor Yinger emphasizes, that a study of minority groups is a study of a social problem that has its origins in the structure and functioning of a society and the place of values in human groups.

Stratification is the basic organizational characteristic of societies. In its simplest terms it means that some people are leaders and others are followers. Man has devised ingenious ways of ordering individuals in status hierarchies with differential rewards and responsibilities, with the objective of accomplishing those things which are necessary if the society is to persist over time. Individuals so ordered become identified with certain groups, and the tendency is to "institutionalize" the organizational arrangements because it "gets the job done" and because those who are leaders and in high status want to keep it that way. They have power and its attendant rewards, and enjoy them.

Differentiation precedes and then accompanies stratification. In any society, specialized jobs are requisite to the society's survival and to its adjustment and adaptation to the social changes occurring both within and outside the society. To meet the demands of differentiation, a society must train its members, especially the talented, in jobs appropriate to the individual's abilities, motivations, and aspirations.

Stratification and differentiation, with its unequal distribution of things considered valued and prized, is the basis of minority problems. The minority problem is most obvious when the stratification system is closed and when barriers are erected against equal achievement of positions in the status system. The major barrier is discrimination, and the grounds for it are irrational and paradoxical when one considers the requirements of an open and expanding stratification system.

Why do societies have minority groups and attendant problems? Professor Yinger offers both historical and sociological evidence for the existence and persistence of minority groups and their concomitant problems. Societal change since 1920 has been convulsive and tumultuous. Existing stratification systems have lacked the flexibility to reduce the deviant consequences of minority-group status, namely isolation, alienation, nonutilization of skills, and loss of identification of the segregated members.

Desegregation is occurring, however, in various sectors of the national life. Professor Yinger explores the judicial and legal acts aimed to reduce the disadvantages of being a minority-group member. He also examines the desegregation patterns in the political community and armed forces, in the fields of sports and entertainment, in public accommodations, in employment, education, and religion. He views desegregation as an inevitable social process necessitated by the rapid social changes within the society. Whether desegregation results in integration or not, the successful future of the society is dependent upon a resolution of the paradox of integration and pluralism.

Professor Yinger explores objectively and unemotionally the basic question of how far a society can integrate its disparate groups into a common culture without losing the viable traditions and identifications which originate from ingroup membership. How heterogeneous can a society be without inviting conflict? Will a pluralistic society with its focus on maintaining group traditions and practices create and preserve minority groups and their associated problems of differential opportunities and discrimination against its members? The unique case of Hawaii, with its blend of integration and pluralism in which there is unity in diversity, is presented as a prototype of a functional system for other societies to copy.

The author is aware of the problems of using a structural system in one society simply because it works in another. Hawaii is an illustration still worth examining, especially since it is part of the Union and can be viewed as a "strategic" case for its possible application in other states. Professor Yinger is also aware of the thin line between undesirable segregation and legitimate pluralism. Systematic or total segregation, as well as other forms of exclusion based on hidden purposes, is undesirable. In legitimate pluralism, individuals are joined in a viable tradition and wish for its development and preservation. How to prevent pluralism from perpetuating outgroup behaviors, which include segregation and discrimination, requires further experience and experimentation with strategies.

Strategies using our advanced knowledge, research, and educational experience are suggested by Professor Yinger. Differences in situations and notions of timing in introducing a strategy are explored. The consequences of nonstrategic action and perpetuation of segregation are viewed as detrimental to the stability of the society. Consequences include nationalism among minority groups and alienation of a growing number of disfranchised minorities. This is a book of facts, ideas, theories, and practices; the reader must learn them, assimilate them, and then act in relation to this knowledge.

Marvin B. Sussman

The problems with which this book deals began perhaps five thousand years ago. Through most of the long prehistory of man, the members of a society or tribe were alike in race, language, religion, and culture. The development of stable agricultural economies with food surpluses, however, permitted the growth of cities, specialization, and trade. Then began continuous and extensive contact among the members of different societies. This led in time, through conquest and migration, to the development of larger political units and multigroup societies. Frequently one or more of the groups thus brought together were less powerful than others in the society, less able to protect themselves or to win equality of treatment. They became minority groups, subject to discrimination.

The era of nationalism has been the minority-creating situation par excellence. Nation-states were often built, and are still being built, out of peoples of diverse religion, race, or ethnic origin. To create unity out of such diversity has been a primary task of most large nations. Thus we are concerned here with a question of worldwide interest, even though the focus of our attention is upon the United States.

The study of minority groups is of international significance not only because most nations are made up of persons drawn from different groups but also because of the great increase in international contact and interdependence. While nations deal in various ways with minority-majority relations, the world as a unit is suddenly being confronted with similar problems. If we are to have international stability and peace, we shall have to learn to live with diversity; we shall have to extend the concept of pluralism beyond the boundaries of the nation. Before Marconi, the Wright brothers, and Einstein—or perhaps before Gagarin, Titov, and Glenn—we might have been able to be content with the question: How can the various members of one society live together in trust and co-operation? Now, even as we struggle with it on the national level, this question presses in on us with ever greater urgency on the world level.

We can scarcely hope to deal successfully with the difficult problems associated with contact among diverse nations until we have learned better how to handle the simpler problems within nations. It is my belief that the way in which the affiliation or rejection of racial, religious, and ethnic minorities is worked out within nations will strongly influence our ability to build a world order in which similarities are not coerced and differences do not divide. We are dealing here with one of the great intellectual and moral questions of the day.

Our reference is primarily to Negroes in American society. The causes and consequences of the "Negro revolt" and its reverberations throughout the society demand the careful attention of the student of minority groups. Basic to our interest in this problem, however, is a concern for more general principles of minority-majority relations, for we can understand the forces at work in a particular situation only through a comparative approach dealing with many situations.

Judged against the importance of the topic, these brief essays are entirely inadequate; the theme of each of the chapters deserves a lengthy monograph. What is intended here is only to prompt the reader to further thought and to suggest how the problems might be better approached. In schematic terms, my hope is to focus attention on three questions related to minority groups: Where are we? Where do we want to be? How can we get there?

The first question requires a descriptive and analytic approach. Change in minority-majority relations is so rapid that only continuous and careful study can tell us accurately where we are. The first five chapters deal with this question, after developing some necessary definitions. Although additional descriptive material is found in Chapter 6, it deals more specifically with moral aspects of the topic. There are obvious differences of opinion on the proper goals in intergroup relations. In my judgment there are moral disagreements far more subtle and extensive than those connected with the desirability and speed of desegregation. Important moral questions will remain after desegregation has been carried much further than it has been. Chapters 7 and 8 raise questions of strategy. Our work is incomplete if we know where we are and where we want to go but have no understanding of how to get there. Perhaps on no other question are our commonsense notions so likely to be inadequate. Effective strategy requires intensive study of both individuals and society, for the patterns of intergroup relations are deeply imbedded in us as persons and in our whole institutional structure. If the reading of these essays encourages and assists the reader in the study of the analytic, moral, and strategic questions related to the place of minority groups in a free society, the author will feel well rewarded.

Portions of Chapters 5 and 6 are based on articles which I wrote for the *Antioch Review* ("Integration and Pluralism Viewed from Hawaii," Winter, 1962–1963, pp. 397–410) and for *Sociology and Social Research* ("Desegregation in American Society: The Record of a Generation of Change," July, 1963, pp. 428–445). My thanks to the editors for permission to use this material. Some of the ideas in this essay were first worked out in a memorandum I prepared for the National Conference of Christians and Jews and in the Haynes Foundation lectures which I delivered at Pomona College in December, 1961. I am grateful for the opportunity to revise and extend those ideas here.

J. Milton Yinger

CONTENTS

CHAPTER

THE STUDY OF SOCIETIES
AND SOCIAL PROBLEMS

Imagine what a visitor from outer space might conclude if he attempted to reconstruct the basic quality of human life from a study of a year's headlines and a running tape of a year's newscasts. At the end he would have a long list of stories dealing with murder and theft, fire and crash, riot and skirmish. There would be a few accounts of friendly acts, of negotiations, of goals accomplished; but the overwhelming impression he would have would be one of conflict. How, he might wonder, does this species manage to survive and even to multiply so rapidly?

If he concluded that conflict was of great significance, few of us would be inclined to argue with him. The evidence is too close at hand and too persistent for us to doubt the importance of conflict, and in this essay we will be concerned with one of its most common manifestations. We must remember, however, that headlines and news stories, almost by definition, record the unusual, the bizarre, the dramatic, the "newsworthy" event.

A deeper fact of human life—so common that we take it for

granted—is the intricate network of mutual expectations, the agreed-upon values, the interdependent actions that characterize the normal course of events. How many times in the last few days have you counted upon other persons (on their values and goals and their actions related to those values and goals) for the satisfaction of some need of your own? Think not only of family and friends but of strangers, of persons whom you will never meet or know, but who are involved in some chain of activity important to you. I am not referring to generosity and acts of friendship particularly, although these are part of the situation, but to the steady performance of roles and the linking of roles into the structures necessary for the achievement of most goals.

This is the basic fact with which sociology starts: Human beings everywhere live in societies; their interaction is guided to an important degree by norms, by agreed-upon rules and procedures. Each society has designed ways of teaching these norms to each new generation, so that everywhere the human infant—that "uncultured barbarian"—goes through a long process of training, of socialization. What he is taught in this process is not necessarily good, according to some stated standard of values. In fact, when societies are studied comparatively, wide variations in their standards and norms—their cultures—are clearly revealed. From any given value perspective, therefore, some will be ranked higher than others. But the sociologist acting in his professional capacity does not make such judgments, although as a private individual, of course, he does. He tries to discover what kinds of value codes are associated with what other social facts, and with what consequences for human behavior. It is his task to observe and explain, not to praise or to blame. He may record that in certain social groups, patterns of prejudice are taught, children are "carefully taught" to hate, as the lyric in *South Pacific* puts it. As a student of society, he does not applaud or lament that fact, but tries to understand it.

The place of this neutrality in the scientific study of societies is a controversial and complicated question, so we may be wise to examine it briefly here at the outset. For most social scientists, objectivity is not an ultimate and final position; it is the position they attempt to maintain *during the processes of observation and inter-pretation.* For some few, this may be the largest part of life; to study and explain is their basic goal. For most, however, the scientific process is part of a larger process. It must be carried out as objectively as possible in order that it may make its maximum contribution to the human enterprise. An individual scientist may be devoted wholly to the effort to understand some part of nature, but he gains support from the fact that he is part of a larger endeavor that uses increased understanding to achieve some human goal. A chemist may have few interests beyond the pure research of his laboratory, but he realizes that the growth in chemical knowledge is contributing to the production of new medicines, fabrics, or other materials. He may devote part of his time to such applications of pure knowledge, an indication of his hope that such knowledge may contribute to the solution of some problem.

The same mixture of objectivity and application characterizes social science. In this book, when we are attempting to observe and to interpret, our aim will be to view from a distance, to maintain as much neutrality as possible. There will be no heroes or villains. Sometimes a minority-group member is seen as hateful and inferior; citing an extreme case, one may pull back in revulsion from the violence of a crime committed by a Negro. We shall simply ask, how-ever: Can we go back twenty years in this person's life? Can we see him as an infant? Was there hatred and violence in him then? Did he receive affectionate support from a family? Did the powerful and "significant others" among the dominant group create conditions that gave him self-respect and a sense of justice?

Most of those who read this book have little difficulty in asking such questions and in noting their relevance for understanding the adult. Are we equally prepared to understand the prejudice or the cruel act of a white man or woman? In New Orleans a few years ago, when the first schools were being desegregated, crowds of white women gathered near the entrances to jeer the Negro children, to spit upon their parents, to stone those few white persons who sought to aid the children, to scream curses at all who disagreed with them. These "cheer leaders," as they came to be called, in their wrinkled dresses, with unkempt hair and wild stares, were the targets of a great deal of moral indignation around the country. Yet once again we must ask: Can we go back in these persons' lives to the conditions of their formative years? Is the hatred in them as infants? Has life promised them much, but given them little? Did they invent the culture of prejudice that tells them whom to hate?

Our task is to observe many facts of nature which may profoundly disturb us without losing our desire to study them simply as facts. Once we have some mastery of them, some confidence that our judgments will not be seriously distorted by the fatal combination of ignorance and bias, we can reintroduce our values. We can say without apology: These things I like, those I dislike. Even then, however, we will be wise to pay attention to conditions and processes, not to heroes and villains. This is a difficult position to hold to. Most of the informal principles of explanation that we learn in the process of growing up attribute the causes of things to persons. It is difficult not to "know," if one follows the news, that James Hoffa has formed the Teamsters' Union into a powerful instrument of coercion—happily or unhappily, depending upon our values. In my judgment it is much more accurately stated, however, that the structural conditions of the transportation system being what they are, a substantial body of power is available to any organization capable of coordinating the responses of transportation workers. Nature abhors not only a physical but a power vacuum. If Hoffa were not head of the Teamsters, someone else with basically similar, but not identical, tendencies would be doing nearly the same things with reference to the public and the transportation companies.

This does not mean, of course, that individuals make no difference. It means that their influence is expressed within limits set by major institutional and cultural forces. These forces do not disappear if we disregard them; by such disregard we simply reduce our ability to understand the scene before us. In the study of minority-majority relations, which is our topic, it is particularly important that we be alert to the ways in which they are embedded in the system of social relationships which we call society.

The Sociology of Social Problems

To stress that social life is characterized to an important degree by reciprocal expectations is not to deny that there are problems, conflicts, and disagreements. But it is important to see those problems, conflicts, and disagreements in perspective, against the background of social order and, indeed, in part the product of social order. This statement requires some interpretation.

It scarcely needs arguing that all societies have problems—hunger, disease, natural disasters, interpersonal conflict. Modern complex societies have reduced some of these (although they have increased others), but they are faced with a still different type of problem. If the food supply of a community is destroyed by drought or storm, everyone is likely to agree that the situation is most unfortunate. If they further agree on what to do about it—perhaps to send every available vehicle to bring food from communities outside the area of damage—they have a technical, but not a social problem. The only question is the adequacy of the means available. But suppose some of the residents declare: The lack of food is no problem; it is good for our souls or our health, or it is a sign from God which we should attempt to read, not to obscure by seeking food elsewhere. There is now a conflict of values, not just a shortage of food—a social dimension has been added. Or perhaps all agree that the shortage of food is a serious problem, but the suggestion that surplus from neighboring communities be sought may be attacked by some who say: Better to go hungry than to get our food from *them;* or, We'll just have to get along, because we cannot go into debt any further. This is a different kind of conflict of values—agreement on ends, but disagreement on means—but it is still a social, and not simply a technical, problem. The basic principle here is that *social problems have social origins,* in the sense that they involve disagreements among the members of the group in question over means or ends or both.[1]

You may think that the illustration I have used is too improbable

NOTE: Footnoted references, numbered consecutively by chapter, appear at the end of the book, pp. 131–137.

to be of much use. Can you think of analogous situations that are more realistic? Does not one find in America today, for example, disagreement over both ends and means with respect to unemployment? Some persons say—although more by actions than by words: Unemployment is not such a bad idea; it keeps workers on their toes; it furnishes a desirable flexibility to the labor force; it reduces inflationary pressures; and besides, it actually hits only those who show little initiative. Most persons would probably disagree with those statements, but so long as they are believed by some—especially by influential people—it is not possible to say that unemployment is simply a technical problem, involving the scarcity of means to a universally accepted goal. There are, in addition, "values in conflict."[2]

More commonly there is agreement on the undesirability of a state of affairs, but disagreement on the remedy. And the disagreements arise to an important degree from the fact that remedies for difficulties in one aspect of society involve other social values and processes. If the cure is worse than the disease, we don't send for the doctor. Unemployment is bad, some may say, but if the only way to reduce it is to spend more public money on education or retraining to lift the level of skill, or on public works, or to eliminate restrictions on minority-group workers—if we must have an unbalanced budget—then we shall have to put up with it. Note that each of these alternatives involves values and institutions. Such disagreements over means are partly the result of a lack of adequate knowledge about the consequences of various strategies. The total long-run impact on unemployment of a massive campaign to improve our educational system is not easy to demonstrate. If we knew more, we would argue less. A developed social science, therefore, can contribute to the reduction of social problems. Some of the disagreement, however, is based on a clash of values. Such issues are not solved, but are struggled with by pulling and hauling among contending groups. Resolutions are temporary, as new forces enter the scene and the effects of past decisions begin to be felt. In time a greater measure of agreement on values may be reached, for the original clash of values may have arisen from a difference in the timing of significant experiences. As different parts of the population catch up, shifts in standards of value will reduce the area of conflict.

These principles clearly apply to minority-majority relations and to the segregation and discrimination which are their major manifestations. Almost everyone agrees that there is "a significant discrepancy between social standards and social actuality," to use Merton's definition of a social problem.[3] But there is sharp disagreement over causes and remedies. Some say: Segregation is not bad, but good; we have trouble today because Negroes, for example, have forgotten their place and have been goaded by agitators into making unwise demands. Others, of course, are convinced that segregation is bad and that it brings a host of further difficulties. Even among these, however, there may be disagreement over remedies. Should we rely on education and appeals to good will, or are the compulsions of law and the picket line desirable? There are many different points of view.

The study of minority groups, then, is the study of a social problem. To understand it requires that one examine the workings of society and the place of values in human action. Our first task will be to stand back from the problem to study the contending forces and the social structures involved. Then we will be able to state our values simply and try to discover what actions are best designed to bring them about.

2

SOCIAL STRATIFICATION:

the basis of minority-majority relations

Most human groups, whether they have two members or many millions, are characterized by social differentiation. The members hold different positions, have different rights and responsibilities, and possess different kinds of influence over group action. In many instances this variation expresses a ranking system; individuals are not only different, but higher and lower, lords and peasants, chiefs and Indians. If this ranking system persists over a period of time, so that there is opportunity for it to be built into institutional patterns and to influence significantly the personalities of the individuals involved, we speak of a particular kind of social differentiation: stratification.

Speaking technically, we will refer to social stratification only if a ranking system lasts more than one generation, only if individuals tend to pass their rank on to their children. Many human associations involve differences in power and status which are more or less temporary, perhaps even momentary: in a bridge game, the person who wins the bid may declare the trump and generally dominates the hand.

On the other hand, the difference may last for years, as in a school, where the greater knowledge of the teacher puts him in a position of leadership, but where the aim is to eliminate the differential. Such variations in rank have very different consequences from those that occur when status is fixed and to an important degree inherited. A bridge game would clearly be quite different if one person had the privilege of always declaring the trump, and it took a revolution to change the rules.

Ranking systems that persist through more than one generation do not simply characterize the interactions of particular individuals, of course, because with their deaths such systems would disappear. Social stratification is a quality of groups, especially of societies. It is passed along, primarily through the family system, by the assignment of each individual to a place in the status structure. Thus in stratified societies—which means most societies—one knows even before a child is born where he will be placed in the ranking system. (This is not, of course, the same as knowing whether he will remain there.) This stratification may seem quite unfair to you—it does to me—but before we can effectively explore the moral problems involved in such a social arrangement, we need to be well informed about its types, its causes, and its consequences. It would be quite ineffective to set out to discover villains and heroes. Social stratification is unfair in the same sense that it is unfair that some persons are struck down by cancer at age three or twenty or forty-five. If we can explore stratification as a natural phenomenon, seeking to understand the social and individual forces with which it is interrelated, we may achieve some ability to control those consequences of it which we believe to be unfortunate.

Summarizing the distinctions drawn here, we can classify groups in the following way:

I. Groups in which all members have similar functions and status (perhaps a small friendship group, although even there some differentiation is common)
II. Groups characterized by differentiation
   A. Unranked differentiation (the workmen on an assembly line,

or an athletic team with its different positions; informal ranking often develops in such groups)

B. Ranked differentiation

   1. "Temporary" (teacher-student relationships or a group
      with elected officials)

   2. "Permanent" (caste systems, societies with majority and
      minority groups, class systems)

We shall be concerned only with the last category in this list, in
fact, only with that kind of "permanent" stratification system associated with majorities and minorities. ("Permanent" and "temporary"
have been put in quotation marks to emphasize that we are actually dealing, not with two distinct types, but with a range which
varies from momentary leadership to fixed social structures that persist almost unchanged through several centuries.) We need to distinguish carefully among the varieties of stratification systems, to
examine their similarities and differences. First, some general questions about social stratification should be considered.

If stratification means unequal distribution of things that are
prized and scarce, we need to know what those things are. There
are three basic types: Income (control over economic goods and
services), prestige (control over social honor), and power (control
over the activities of other persons).[1] These are closely related, of
course, but not identical. One of the most important things you
can know about a society or about an individual is the extent to
which income, prestige, and power are distributed in similar or dis-
similar ways. When an individual has the same ranking on each
of the various scales, he is said to have a "crystallized status." When
his ranks are different from one scale to the other, his status is
"uncrystallized." This is not an either-or question, of course, but a
variable that can range from complete or nearly complete identity
of ranks to situations of extreme diversity. The degree of a person's
status crystallization is an important aspect of his experience and
influences his behavior in significant ways. There is evidence, for
example, that a highly uncrystallized status is associated with those
who are liberal in politics, particularly if they rank high in edu-

cation and in occupational position, but low in "social honor"— perhaps as a result of minority-group membership. Other combinations may be associated with different results; high ethnic or racial rank, for example, coupled with low educational and occupational rank may produce high rates of psychological disturbance.[2]

Status inconsistency is also important for the society. A society in which those with high income also have high prestige and power tends to be a stable—or static—society; individuals within it tend to regard the arrangements as natural and inevitable. Even those on the bottom are much more likely to be concerned with finding a comfortable or honorable situation *at their accustomed level* than with trying to change levels or to attack the system. If there is a sense of injustice, it is likely to be expressed in religious terms which redefine the meaning of their status without attempting to change it. They are quite unable to change their status, lacking, as they do, income, prestige, and power.

Those who are on top in such an arrangement are naturally disposed to regard it as a desirable, natural, and honorable arrangement. They may be thoughtful and generous with those who are less well placed; there may, indeed, be a strong tradition of obligation on their part, a sense of *noblesse oblige,* to protect the customary rights of "their" peasants, serfs, slaves, or workers and to treat them with personal generosity. This does not reflect, however, any lack of support for the stratification system.

The situation is quite different when income, prestige, and power become separated. A lowly person finds gold; a religious prophet discovers that those who hear him are ready to work for a new society; a frustrated ex-serviceman, as Hitler was, discovers that his discontent with life is matched by that of many others who are ready to follow his lead; or technical inventions or migration open new economic opportunities. Such circumstances bring severe pressures to bear on the established stratification systems.

Persons without prestige or power may find themselves with high income; or persons without income or prestige may find themselves with power. Then they become unwilling to accept the old arrangements. In the same circumstances, some of those who formerly possessed income, prestige, and power may find one or more of these values fading—inherited wealth used up or the basis of their power swept away by social change.

All of this is to say that under many conditions, including particularly the highly mobile and changing conditions of modern societies, individuals and groups are constantly widening or narrowing their claims upon the scarce values of life. Stratification systems become highly complex and dynamic. The effects of change reach out far beyond the particular individuals whose status becomes uncrystallized. When this happens to some, it becomes apparent also to others that the prevailing distribution of life's values is not part of an inevitable order of things. Ideologies develop which may spread to those who are still personally at the bottom of the ladder. To Weber's basic three values, therefore, let us add two others: dreams and hope. If those who lack income, power, and prestige have caught a dream of something different because some of their fellows have demonstrated the possibility of change, their status becomes uncrystallized in their imaginations, if not in fact.

"I have a dream," Martin Luther King said to the 210,000 persons who stood before him in Washington, D.C., one August day in 1963. "I have a dream"—an explosive phrase, for it echoed throughout the crowd and throughout the land; and millions of Negroes still without power or prestige and with little income looked at life differently. A fully crystallized stratification system must distribute dreams as unequally as it distributes other values if it is to remain unchanged.

Dreams, however, are not the same as hope. There can be dreams without hope, but not hope without dreams. It is very important to imagine the consequences of their separation. They probably appear together when persons near the bottom of a stratification system begin to experience some rise in status and learn about others who have risen even further. After a time, however, they may run into serious resistance to their further advance. (American Negroes, for example, made steady economic gains from 1940 to about 1953; but in the next decade, there was little further improvement. The protest movement of the 1960s is partly a reflection of that fact.) Their dreams do not fade, at least not quickly; but hopes of continuing realization are dampened. Such a situation is almost certain to promote strong opposition to the prevailing stratification system, the type of opposition varying with many things. If the process of change which leads to the increased hope in the first place produces a fairly significant increase in income among the lower strata and an increase in power (perhaps by bettering their education), opposition may take the form of the current civil rights movement among American Negroes—a strong effort to modify the stratification system, but largely within the framework of the existing ideology. If, on the other hand, there has been a much larger component of dreams than of hope—as among the unskilled and poorly educated Negroes in the urban slums—the protest may take a more drastic form. Frustration may lead to demoralization and an attack on one's self, such as alcoholism or mental illness; to an individual repudiation of the society, or criminality; or to an organized repudiation of society, such as the Black Muslims.

We will come back to various aspects of this question at several points in later chapters. Here I want only to get you to imagine the various possible outcomes of stratification systems that distribute life's scarce values in different ways. Schematically, and leaving out the actual complexities of the situation, one may sketch the situation among American Negroes in the following way:

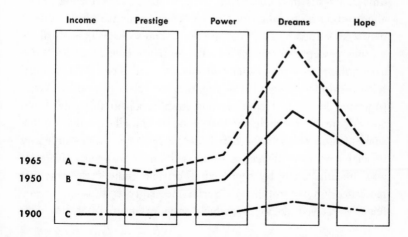

Whether or not these rough guesses are near the mark, they may indicate the point that one of the central questions one needs to ask about a stratification system concerns its distribution of these values and the direction of change in the pattern of distribution.

The distribution of scarce values is always partly comparative. Prestige and power, in fact, are always in scarce supply, since if one person or group has them, others must, by definition, be without them. Income is not comparative in such a rigid sense; yet our responses are strongly affected by our relative position. A $5,000 income means one thing if it places a person in the top third of all the workers in his society; it is something quite different, even if it will purchase the same goods and services, if it places him in the bottom third. Because of this comparative quality, it is necessary to relate the brief description of lack of status crystallization among Negroes to the facts concerning various groups of whites—the farmer in a declining agricultural region, the lower-middle-class family which has just bought its first house outside the deteriorated area of a city, and others. It is in the interplay among the groups experiencing widely different types of gain and threat that the processes of race relations are worked out.

Sources of Social Stratification

By now you have doubtless asked yourself: Why are societies so universally stratified? Mankind seems to be so experimental about almost everything, when one views societies comparatively, that it may seem surprising that there are not several societies that distribute income, power, and prestige equally, or, if not equally, at least give each infant an equal chance to compete for them. When social scientists find a universal structure, they are likely to wonder: What functions does it perform? Viewing stratification in this way, Davis and Moore have concluded that it occurs in all societies for the simple reason that stratification is necessary to get various necessary societal jobs done. Talent is scarce; certain critical jobs which are also difficult might be neglected if capable individuals were not motivated to perform them. "Social inequality is thus an unconsciously evolved device by which societies insure that the most important positions are conscientiously filled by the most qualified persons."[3] This begins to answer the question, but there are many problems it does not solve. How much of a reward is needed to motivate the right persons to do the essential tasks? In the United States today, for example, some people make a thousand dollars a day, a few make as much as ten thousand dollars a day, but many make less than a thousand dollars a year. Is that much differential required? In commenting on the functional theory, Dennis Wrong notes that "it in no way denies that a particular distribution of rewards prevailing in a given historical society may vastly exceed the minimum inequalities necessary to maintain a complex division of labor. Nor does it deny that some roles that are unimportant, unskilled, and pleasurable may be highly rewarded provided only that they do not compete so successfully with roles possessing the opposite attributes that they reduce the quantity or the quality of candidates for the latter below some minimum level."[4]

Functional requirements, then, may give the differential system of rewards a slight start, but the system soon becomes self-perpetuating. Remember that a central characteristic of stratification is its permanence.[5] Those who are in favorable positions are well placed to ensure that their children get a head start. Perhaps this is an essential advantage to ensure highest motivation: one works harder because he knows his children will benefit thereby. But this easy answer runs into a serious difficulty: What happens to the motivation of those who see how *little* they can pass on to their children? That which ensures good performance from some may discourage it in others.

The functional explanation of stratification, in short, is only a beginning. To it must be added a power explanation: Stratification exists because some persons, partly because of their functional contributions, perhaps, and partly by chance, have attained superior income, power, and prestige, and these resources give them the necessary instruments for maintaining their position. Under conditions of rapid change, the position is by no means entirely secure, as we have noted. Persons with *some* advantages, but not the most, may be more vigorous in the pursuit of scarce values than those at the top. The old adage, "three generations from shirt sleeves to shirt sleeves," is not without some truth; yet alongside it must be put the homely truth that the best way to be successful is to pick a successful father. Lacking that, it is wise to pick a society in which the ideology and the institutional patterns emphasize public advantages, particularly education, for all.

Types of Stratification Systems

This leads us to a third question about stratification systems:

How do societies vary in the degree to which they are open or closed? This is not the same as asking about the extent of status crystallization, although the two questions are closely related. Openness refers to the ease and frequency with which individuals change status. If everybody remained on the status level of his parents, a system would be completely closed; if everybody moved to a level different from his parents, higher or lower, the system would be completely open. Neither of these extremes is found in practice, although some societies are fairly nearly closed. We do well to think of this as a continuum, not as a situation characterized by three or four sharply contrasting types. Since there is evidence that in modern industrial societies approximately one-third of the people rise above or fall below their parents' status[6] and that there was little change of status in the classic Indian caste system,[7] we might use these as the *empirical* ends of the range and compare them with the theoretically possible range:

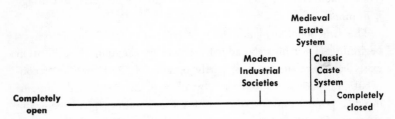

Since a completely open system by our definition, however, would be a topsy-turvy world in which everybody who was up went down and everybody who was down went up, we might get a more accurate picture of the reasonably possible range by considering 50 percent mobility to be the maximum degree of openness. Our range would then look like this:

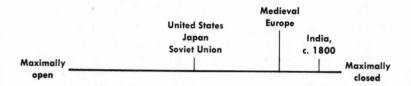

Note that even societies as different as the United States and the Soviet Union can have nearly the same degree of social mobility. This indicates that urbanization and industrialization, rather than ideology, seem to be the key factors in determining the rate of social mobility.

We stated above that the degree of openness of a status system was not the same as the extent of its status crystallization. It is possible for an individual to move up or down on all of the various scales at the same rate; e.g., his income, prestige, and power might all go up by about the same amount. This would mean that his status would remain crystallized even while he experienced social mobility. Oppositely, a person might have an uncrystallized status—perhaps high prestige, but low income and power—and remain at the same level. Nevertheless it is probably true that closed societies are very likely to be characterized by a much higher degree of status crystallization than open societies.

The degree to which a society is open or closed is not fixed, of course. One of the most important considerations in an attempt to understand a society is the direction of its development in this regard. The evidence is not easy to weigh. There is sharp disagreement, for example, regarding trends in the United States. Is the country more open than it was, let us say in 1900; is it more likely that a poor boy will rise, and that a privileged boy will fall, in status? Or is it more closed, with greater barriers to advancement and more protections against loss? Or has there, perhaps, been little change? I do not know how to answer this question definitively, but perhaps the issues involved may be examined by imagining a debate between someone who believes the society is more open and someone who believes it is more closed:

More open

1. A society with a closed class system has a clear "power elite" —a group that dominates all the major institutions. But since 1900, there has been a significant growth of labor unions, governmental control agencies, and other "countervailing powers."

2. American income is distributed in a more equalitarian way than it was in 1900. The top 20 percent gets a smaller proportion of the total.

3. Style of life—fashion, special clothing for different occasions, speech differences—all separate classes less now than formerly.

4. The race line is drawn far less sharply now. Negroes are being educated in large numbers and there is now a large Negro middle class.

5. Changes in our economy have created a much higher proportion of middle-class jobs. Many more individuals have climbed than need to fall.

6. America has experienced a truly dramatic increase in educational opportunity since 1900. Inexpensive education through the university level is accessible to a very high proportion.

More closed

1. The cold war, the rise of mammoth industries, the inaccessibility of "big government" to most people have caused a reduction of flexibility, a concentration of power.

2. Perhaps, but the evidence is scanty. More millionaires are being made today than ever before. Expense-account living is difficult to measure.

3. But new modes of differentiation take their places: travel, expensive forms of recreation, training in the arts.

4. This cannot be doubted, but neither can the persisting reality of discrimination. And the gap between what Negroes have and what they hope for is probably greater now, not smaller.

5. This gain must be seen alongside the fact of persistent unemployment for millions and the devastating effects of automation.

6. True, but there are still gaps in *quality* and a great failure to make accessible those educational opportunities that match the existing economic opportunities. Colleges are class stratified, and to some degree help to perpetuate the system.

This debate could go on at much greater length. We might continue it briefly by shifting the lead of the argument from the open to the closed side. Now read the right-hand column first.

7. But the continuing development of new industries is a modern frontier.

7. With the closing of the frontier, in the late nineteenth century, America lost her major force for an open society.

8. The large amount of internal mobility, particularly the shift from farms to the city, produces much the same effect.

8. The great flow of immigrants into the United States was a major factor in her open class system. Each new group lifted the others up a notch. This is now sharply curtailed.

9. But the large bureaucracies open many jobs to persons of low-prestige origins by their processes of rational, objective selection, civil service examinations, and the like.

9. We now have an old, established elite; a mature economy; mammoth corporations with vast advantages over any possible new competitor. The small businessman or small company now has little chance of success.

It is, indeed, a complicated question. My own judgment is that the United States is slightly more open than it was in 1900. Arguments 4, 5, and 6, above, seem to me to be decisive in this regard, even though there are significant influences on the other side. Whether or not my judgment is correct, it is important to weigh the evidence, because this question is crucial to understanding a society and, more specifically, is vital to the study of minority groups.[8]

There are many other questions that deserve attention in connection with social stratification: To what degree are individual members class-conscious, that is, aware of their placement, and what are the consequences of various degrees of awareness? What is the level of conflict among strata? What aspects of a society make it likely that conflict will be frequent or infrequent? How is the stratification system linked with other parts of the society? Since this is a basic sociological question, we will examine it briefly. Lipset and

Bendix note, for example, the connections between religious beliefs, the family, and stratification:

Cultures which emphasize success require that individuals be able to adjust to personal failure. A number of mechanisms may serve this need, of which two that seem particularly important in America may be briefly suggested here: (1) transvaluational religion, which teaches that the good rather than the rich will be rewarded in an afterlife; and (2) a high degree of child-centeredness that encourages parents to seek satisfaction in high aspirations for their children when their own personal goals have not been achieved. Both may be viewed as means of safeguarding society against instability. In America, for example, the depressed strata seem to have turned to evangelical religion rather than to radical politics; in Russia, where political protest is forbidden, there is also some evidence of "a return to religion" among the poorer strata; and both societies—each in its own way—seem to place an extraordinarily high emphasis on a better life for children. It is in the societies of Europe and Asia where less emphasis is placed on equality of opportunity that leftwing political movements are strong among the lower strata— presumably because they teach that traditional inequities can be done away with by changing the social system.[9]

All of this is to say that in studying the stratification system of a society, whether in general, or with the particular interest with which we will now examine the place of minority groups in it, one must at the same time study many other important questions about that society.

3

MINORITY GROUPS, CASTES, AND CLASSES

In the preceding chapter we have noted that most societies are not only differentiated, but stratified. The rewards of a society are distributed unequally, and this inequality is built into the structure of its institutions so that it tends to persist from one generation to the next. In observing that societies could be placed along a range from open to closed, we oversimplified the picture in order to get a basis for comparison. Now we need to add some of the complexities which we left out. These complexities include the relationship of stratification to other social structures, such as religion, politics, and the law; the influence of major cultural values; and the attitudes of individual participants.

This book is primarily about minority groups and their relationships to majority groups. Why do we need these terms? Why not speak simply of lower, middle, and upper classes, or use some variation of that terminology? Are minority groups castes? Or, more adequately, is there sufficient variation in that part of nature we are trying to understand to make it wise to use two terms? We are dealing with complex distinctions, hence we must proceed with some care. It may be well to begin with a formal definition, this one taken from Louis Wirth:

We may define a minority as a group of people who, because of their physical or cultural characteristics, are singled out from the others in the society in which they live for differential and unequal treatment, and who therefore regard themselves as objects of collective discrimination.[1]

"Differential and unequal treatment" does not necessarily mean that one is at the bottom. If two well-trained and competent persons compete for a job of high prestige and income, and one loses out *on the grounds of his group membership alone,* this does not indicate a low-class status, but rather a minority-group status. A minority is a group which, regardless of where it is on the class ladder, faces barriers to the pursuit of life's values that are greater than the barriers faced by persons otherwise equally qualified. This is a distinction superimposed on the class system. A member of a minority group, then, is not necessarily lower class, but he is lower on the stratification ladder than he would be were it not for his group membership. One can think of this as a particular kind of status discrepancy or lack of crystallization.

Putting the issue in simple mathematical terms, one can think of scores assigned on the basis, for example, of occupational prestige, income, education, and group membership. Thus a Negro physician with equivalent income and training would fall below a white physician in those situations where race is considered important. His score might be $10 + 10 + 10 + 1$, while his white colleague received a rating of $10 + 10 + 10 + 10$. Group membership may, in fact, be weighted so much more heavily than the others that the Negro physician is ranked below the white unskilled laborer, as if the scores ran $10 + 10 + 10 + 1$ and $1 + 1 + 1 + 50$.[2] In a Detroit suburb a few years ago, the residents actually designed a rating system that prevented a Jewish doctor from getting enough points to allow him to buy a house there, despite the high prestige of his occupation and the level of his training, but did not bar several non-Jewish gangsters from building palatial homes there.[3]

Minority-group status, then, is not the same thing as lower-class status. This is not to suggest, however, that the two are unrelated, for there is no doubt that the disprivileges faced by members of minority groups are sometimes so severe that most of them are kept at the bottom of the class ladder. As is so often true when one is thinking about a complex question, one must distinguish two concepts analytically while recognizing their close empirical connection.

A somewhat similar situation exists in the relationship between caste and minority group. The latter certainly has castelike qualities—more so under some conditions than others—but there are also important marks of difference. Perhaps we can define caste in terms of four characteristics: A caste is characterized by *affiliation by descent,* that is, one is born into a caste, as contrasted with *affiliation by validating behavior.* Castes are endogamous; that is, one must marry within the caste. Individuals in a caste system characteristically accept their status, whether high or low, as appropriate.[4] And the status hierarchy of a caste system is supported and validated by the institutions of the society—the political, occupational, religious, familial, and other structures.

Each of these criteria must be put on a scale of more or less: none is a yes-or-no question. This means that there can be mixed types and ambiguous situations. Disregarding these complexities, however, we can say that a class system contrasts with a caste system on all four of the measures. One's class affiliation is determined more by behavior than by descent; a strict rule of endogamy does not prevail, even though most marriages are intraclass; individuals in a class system may look upon their status as undesirable and unjust and seek to change it; and the institutions of an open class society support the idea of mobility, of change of status, of placement on the basis of individual merit not of inheritance.

A minority-majority situation, on the other hand, tends to be similar to the caste situation on two counts and different on the other two. The rule of descent applies to both: one is "born into" a minority or majority group, just as he is born into a caste; and endogamy is the rule for both, although slightly less so for the minority-majority situation. Minorities, however, do not regard their situation as just and acceptable; nor does the discrimination implied in the concept of minority, the differential and unequal treatment, receive support from the basic institutions of society. There may be some support, but the fundamental rules of law and the basic religious ideology oppose discrimination. In these two respects, therefore, a minority-majority situation is similar to a class system.

In pure "type" terms, disregarding the ambiguities that actually prevail, we can state the relationship among these three patterns of stratification in this way:

	Affiliation by descent	Endogamy	Institutional support for differential treatment	Acceptance of status by lower groups
Caste system	yes	yes	yes	yes
Minority-majority system	yes	yes	no	no
Class system	no	no	no	no

This is actually too simple an arrangement, because it fails to show that each of these qualities can be present in varying amounts. Let us imagine that each might range from 0 to 100. If the four scales were put side by side, we would get not three but many types of stratification systems, perhaps as follows:

		Affiliation by descent	Endogamy	Institutional support for differential treatment	Acceptance of status by lower groups
Caste systems	a	100	100	100	100
	b	100	100	100	90
	c	100	100	90	80
Minority-majority systems	a	100	100	80	70
	b	100	90	70	60
	c	90	80	60	50
Class systems	a	80	70	50	40
	b	70	60	40	30
	c	60	50	30	20
	d	50	40	20	10

For convenience we could call the first three combinations types of caste systems, the next three majority-minority systems, and the last four class systems; but the emphasis would be on the lack of sharp distinctions among types. When societies change in one or more of the four criteria, we are often puzzled about their proper classification. Is India still a caste system, now that many of the former disprivileges of the lower groups are legally prohibited (this has not eliminated them of course) and many persons there protest their status?[5] Perhaps she has become a caste system type c, rather than a, or has moved into the type a minority-majority situation. In some liberal communities in the Northern part of the United States, race relations are perhaps near to class system type a, while in the rural South the more accurate specification may be minority-majority system, type a.

This "quantification" should not be taken too seriously. Perhaps other variables should be listed in addition to or in place of the four suggested. The patterns of decline that I have listed may not be the most likely ones, although I believe they fit the evidence of many societies. The important point is that types of stratification systems vary along a number of dimensions that can combine in many different ways. You might well improve upon the scheme I have suggested here by learning all you can about a particular society to see where it falls on each of these measures and what the patterns of change are. In the process, you will learn a great deal about the whole structure of that society.

Discrimination

The central focus of our attention from now on will be upon minority groups, but we shall keep in mind that they shade off on one side toward castes and on the other side toward classes. Wherever there are minority groups, there is, by definition, discrimination. This is an ambiguous word, however, and we need to define it carefully. The dictionary says that discrimination is the power of "acute discernment," which is a quality we all like to have. To tell the difference between a concerto well played and one poorly played, a basketball maneuver skillfully executed and one clumsily done, a gourmet meal and plainer fare, are sorts of discrimination we work hard to acquire. The dictionary also defines discrimination, however, as "an unfair or injurious distinction"— almost an opposite meaning. The white person is admitted to the school but the Negro is not; a non-Jewish racketeer can buy a home in the neighborhood, to cite our earlier example, but a Jewish doctor cannot. One quality of discrimination is the tendency to treat unequal people equally—that is, to treat all members of the minority group as if they were alike. But if all persons of Mexican descent, or all Chinese, or all persons from Mississippi look alike to us and receive identical treatment regardless of their individual qualities, it is clear that we have deprived ourselves of the power of acute discernment which is the first meaning of discrimination. I shall not try to interpret here why a word should have such contrasting meanings, but will simply note that in the context of this book discrimination will always mean the application of standards which are arbitrary and unfair by dominant standards. The central meaning of "minority group" to those who are thus identified is precisely that they are judged by standards which are in violation of major social values.

Discrimination is easier to define than it is to use as a precise concept. It implies that criteria are used which are not culturally acceptable; but most societies, perhaps all societies that have minority groups, have a wide range of cultural criteria. There are different standards in different regions and classes and occupations. To keep Negroes out of a school which is close to their house may violate the standards and laws of New York, but it is in harmony with the laws and customs of Alabama. Which criteria should one use in determining whether or not school segregation is a form of discrimination? Here your judgment as a student of society has to be brought into play. What are the fundamental values of the society in question? Which laws take precedence according to constitution and practice? How do the members of the minority group feel about it (for they, too, belong to the society)? Do all of those who support segregation believe in it thoroughly, or are some of them doing the thing expected in their community, or are they ambivalent? These are difficult questions. They are more difficult because in a rapidly changing society, yesterday's answer may not be accurate today; and the pressures toward change hit different groups at different times. In fact, discrimination always has some support—or it wouldn't be a subject of study—even though it violates the dominant standards. Disagreement, therefore, is implicit in the very concept.

In my judgment, differential treatment *solely on the grounds of race, religion, national origin, ethnic group, class, age, or sex* is in violation of the dominant American value system and legal structure and is therefore discrimination. This does not mean, of course, that refusal to grant a thirteen-year-old boy a driver's license or hesitation in the employment of a woman crane operator is discrimination. Presumably there are grounds of strength, size, and experience which have been determinative and simply happen to be correlated in these instances with age and sex.

Even purely arbitrary distinctions that use group membership as the deciding factor are not discrimination if they represent the dominant values. Thus the severe burdens imposed on the outcastes in India during the period of its established caste system—however repugnant they may seem to us—were not discrimination in the sense in which we are using the word. They are only beginning to become so as Indian law and custom change.

By this discussion it should be apparent that discrimination is a descriptive term, not a moral evaluation. It becomes a moral term also for any person when he states his own fundamental values and measures the degree to which given acts of differential treatment violate them. This you are encouraged to do. But it is essential first to make a clear distinction between the use of the term as a descriptive concept and as a moral judgment.

The Origin of Minorities

How does it come about that the members of some groups are set apart for unequal treatment? It is not difficult to imagine why this is done to some individuals. They may have some peculiar talent for antagonizing others (perhaps a perfectly good talent, by some standards) and thus miss out on things for which they are fully qualified. But discrimination occurs when all members of a group are treated in a manner that is in violation of accepted standards no matter what characteristics they possess as individuals. The origin of this practice is to be found in the appearance of heterogeneous societies. Through most of man's history—the first several hundred thousand years of it—he lived in small, homogeneous societies. All members spoke the same language, practiced the same religion, were of the same physical type, and followed the same customs. A few thousand years ago this situation began to change as a result of migration and conquest. Groups which were different in important ways came into continuous contact. Under some circumstances they were formed into larger structures—nations and empires. Their former identities, however, frequently remained. There were conquerors and conquered; tribes clung to their own customs and religions—the sacred ways of their fathers; racial lines remained; memories of an earlier day when they had been independent stood as barriers against loss of group identity.[6]

Today, both migration and the process of forging larger societies continue to create minorities. There is scarcely a society in the world today that does not have within it one or more groups, different in language, religion, race, or culture, which are in some measure disprivileged. Most of the new African nations are congeries of tribes, one or a few of which may dominate the others. The Soviet Union includes literally hundreds of different groups which can be distinguished—and distinguish themselves—on the basis of language, religion, ethnic group, or cultural origin. Although the Soviet constitution and ideology support equality of treatment, traditional antipathies and present manipulations of prejudice for political purposes lead to discrimination.[7] The dominant European population of New Zealand first fought the native tribesmen, the Maoris, then sought to protect them, and now find themselves in conflict over land ownership and differences in custom—a situation quite similar to the relationship between American Indians and the dominant whites. From a distance we tend to see China as one vast, homogeneous land. In actual fact, there are many ethnic, lingual, and religious minorities within her borders which constitute less than 10 percent of the population but occupy much more than 10 percent of the land. They are often less than enthusiastic about the central government at Peiping, and become, in turn, the objects of campaigns to eliminate what the federal government calls "regional nationalism." Israel has within her borders an Arab minority, protected by law but highly disprivileged in this predominantly Jewish land; there are also sharp distinctions among the Jews, drawn primarily on the basis of country of origin. Thus Oriental Jews, from the countries of the Near East and North Africa, are regarded with disfavor by many Jews of European origin.[8] In recent years, England has received nearly a quarter of a million colored migrants from various Commonwealth countries, especially Jamaica. Their legal rights have been thoroughly protected, but discrimination in jobs and housing, accentuated by some acts of mob violence, have demonstrated their minority status. As a result of the conflicts and agitation, Great Britain passed, in 1962, her first immigration law curtailing migration from Commonwealth countries.[9] In South Africa, some 3 million white persons utterly dominate the 14 million Africans and persons of Indian descent, which illustrates that a "minority" in sociological terms may be the numerical majority.[10]

These examples are recorded here simply to document the fact that majority-minority situations are very widespread in the modern world. The list is in no sense complete; the student of Japan and Indonesia, of Canada and France, of Brazil and the United States, and of many other lands must be a student of minorities if he is to understand these societies. The simple fact is that in a mobile world where many nations have been formed out of the consolidation of formerly distinctive groups, minority-majority situations occur frequently.

There is some danger that meanings will be read into that last sentence which were not intended. It is not a sigh of resignation that discrimination and group conflict are so deeply entrenched that nothing can be done. It is true that minorities are a natural product of our kind of world. It is also true, however, that there are vast differences in the kinds of discrimination against them—ranging from Hitler's almost incredible campaign of genocide against Jews to the rudiments of a traditional prejudice which has almost disappeared, such as one might find in the United States toward persons of Italian descent. It is important to remember, moreover, that to describe the origin and present status of minorities is not to describe the future. Societies continue to undergo dramatic changes: networks of communication, supported by nearly universal literacy in many lands, create a sense of national identity; social inventions of many kinds, such as laws and intergroup relations commissions, are designed to protect the rights of minorities and to promote intergroup harmony; almost daily demonstrations of the vast interdependence, not only of the groups within a nation, but of the whole world, underline the danger of intergroup conflict; and new ideologies evolve that go beyond earlier pictures of the homogeneous society as the only good society. This last point is one of the most important, and we will deal with it at some length in a later chapter under the topic of pluralism. It has taken us some time to get over the old tribal idea that all members of a society should look alike and think alike. Past or present campaigns of Americanization, Russification, Germanification, or Chinafication have been guided by the idea that variation in language, religion, race, and ethnic identity was injurious to the nation. Minorities were to be assimilated and converted, or encapsulated in some special status (and often territory), or driven out. In the modern world, this is a formula for trouble. And insofar as we carry it over from national to international policy, it is a formula for catastrophe. This question must be given most careful thought.

Types of Minorities

A moment's thought reveals a number of grounds on the basis of which minorities can be classified. Some are of higher than average class, like the Chinese in Thailand or the Jews in the United States; others are of lower than average class, like Jamaicans in England or Negroes in the United States. The symbol or criterion by which they are distinguished may be religion, language, national origin, race, or some combination of these and other characteristics. The group may constitute a very large part of the population, like the Bantu in

South Africa, or a small part, like the Indians in the United States. Each of these considerations influences majority-minority relations. Perhaps the most important system of classification, however, is based on the long-run goals of the minority. Louis Wirth distinguished four such goals: assimilation, pluralism, secession, and domination.[11] Many minority groups are divided on policy, but the primary theme may be: Let us disappear as a group, judge us only as individuals—assimilation; let us maintain our group identity, based perhaps on language, religion, or culture, so long as we give full allegiance to society—pluralism; give us our freedom, let us establish our own society where we can practice our way of life without hindrance—secession; we are weary of being dominated, and we shall do everything we can to reverse the present status arrangement, by militant means if necessary—domination.

To understand a society, it is very important to know the goals of its minorities, the causes of those goals, and the changes that are taking place in them. American minorities have almost always been assimilationist or pluralistic. There has been some secessionism among the Indians and less commonly among Negroes. To some degree the contemporary Black Muslin movement is militant, emphasizing themes of domination, but the three other themes also play some part in its views of the world.[12]

In Europe, the term minority is much more likely to be associated with "a group of people living on soil which they have occupied from time immemorial, but who, through change of boundaries, have become politically subordinate."[13] Such groups are only very slightly assimilationist; they tend to be strongly pluralistic and often secessionist. It is with such groups in mind that the United Nations Subcommission on Prevention and Protection of Minorities uses this definition: ". . . those nondominant groups in a population which possess and wish to preserve stable ethnic, religious or linguistic traditions or characteristics markedly different from those of the rest of the population."[14]

In commenting on the similarities and differences between the French Canadians and Negro Americans, Hughes well demonstrates the importance of distinguishing types of minorities:

The two minorities are alike in that they have gone from a rural condition to an urban and see themselves as thereby put into a position of increased disadvantage. . . . But they see opposite remedies. The Negro Americans want to disappear as a defined group; they want to become invisible as a group, while each of them becomes fully visible as a human being. . . . The French Canadians, on the other hand, struggle not for survival as individuals—in which their problems are those of other Canadians—but for survival as a group with full social, economic, and political standing.[15]

In our study of minority groups, it is important that we keep in mind these distinctions among types. The patterns, however, are not fixed; we must be ready to recognize the signs of change. Moreover, most minorities are to some degree divided on what they believe is the best course, so that we must not assume that each group can be classified without qualification.

Forces Perpetuating Discrimination

To account for the origin of a minority group is not to account for its continuation. A tree that sprouted from an acorn a century ago draws its present life from the water, soil, and air available to it now. What forces sustain discrimination once it has been set in motion? The answer is quite complex, for we must deal with a series of mutually interacting forces woven into a system. Some of these forces may have priority in time, but once they become part of the system, they are best understood as part of an interdependent complex.

The meaning of this statement can perhaps best be explained by sketching a historical sequence: Two groups collide as a result of (1) military conquest, e.g., the Europeans and the American Indians; (2) one group migrating into the territory of the other, e.g., the Mexican immigrants into the United States; or (3) individuals of one group capturing individuals from the other, e.g., the Africans brought to America. In most instances, each group believes itself superior to the other. Such a belief is called ethnocentrism. Because of greater military, economic, or political power, one dominates the other, thus giving one kind of reality to their "superiority." But what happens after this initial contact? It may be helpful to examine this question by noting what happened after the Europeans dominated the American Indians. There were great economic and military advantages to be derived from this domination; these were doubtless the first cause of Indian subjugation. To force them into and keep them in minority status was profitable. This may seem quite crass and unjust, as it probably did to many of the European settlers. They made it seem less unjust, however, not by eliminating the discrimination, but by developing a comforting rationalization: The Indian is a lying, thieving, murdering savage. Not everybody believed this, but it became such a well-established part of the culture that many persons who had never seen an Indian "knew" what all of them were like. Such stereotypes become as much a part of a culture as the rules of etiquette, the esthetic tastes, and the norms of good conduct that each of its members is taught in the process of being socialized to a society.

We have now two basic causes of discrimination and prejudice: economic and military conflict and cultural norms. To these a third is often added. Some individuals in a society carry heavy loads of hostility. Perhaps because life has been cruel to them, their most serious needs for security and affection have been unsatisfied, and their expectations frustrated by neglect or capricious treatment from parents, they have come to believe that the world is a jungle. They have a powerful urge to strike out at a world which has treated them so badly. But they also need security. Therefore, they do not attack those who are powerful or those who are close to them. But if society furnishes them a minority group that is relatively powerless, characterized—so the stereotype teaches them—by evil or inferior ways, and sufficiently different and distant that they feel no attachment to its members, then they can vent their hostility on this group, feeling all the while that they have struck a blow for freedom and justice. Thus, "The only good Indian is a dead Indian." Insofar as hostility results from the neglect and cruelty of one's own group and is transferred to the minority group because it is relatively powerless and alien, we speak of displacement.

A closely related process also arises from the personalities of insecure members of the dominant group. They may feel guilty for things they have done. Hundreds of thousands of Indians were killed by those who were in the process of taking over their land, and many persons doubtless felt guilty about this. Granted the gains made possible by driving the Indians back, however, and the comforting stereotypes about them, this guilt seldom came fully into view. It was deflected, or in technical terms projected, onto someone else: It is not I, it is he who is guilty. Now this is a peculiar mechanism of the human mind, for the projection of dimly felt guilt is almost always onto the very persons whose mistreatment has made us feel guilty. This seems to be a very effective disguise. It is the principle of the "big lie": no one would think of telling a story like that unless it were the truth—yet it reverses the truth. One would almost think that it had been the Indian who had invaded the white man's land, driven him back, cut his population to a third of its original size, unilaterally changed treaties, and brought the dubious glories of firewater and firearms. The pictures of most minority groups are loaded with such projected images. It is interesting to reflect, for example, on the stereotype of the Negro in the minds of many white men: The Negro is aggressive, sexually uninhibited and dangerous, and untrustworthy. If one dispassionately studies the course of history and asks who invaded the other's land, captured millions, transported them with neglectful cruelty into slavery, exploited their women (80 percent of American Negroes have some white ancestry), and cheated them at the company store or in rental overcharge—the answer is beyond question: the white man. His stereotype of the Negro carries many disguised projections of his own guilt.[16]

Thus we have economic conflict, cultural training, and some intricate personality mechanisms reenforcing each other in the thoughts and feelings of majority-group members. But this is still not the whole story. Minority-group members are not passive targets in all of this. They often fight back, in one way or another, increasing the hostility and the sense of "justice" among dominant persons. More important, there are powerful pressures which tend to make minority persons into the kinds of persons the stereotypes say they are. If, on the basis of a belief that they are inferior, one gives to a group poor schools, poor jobs, few opportunities for self-respect, little opportunity for advancement, one soon proves his belief to be correct, for one has created the conditions for its reenforcement. We all acquire our sense of self from the responses of others to us; our images, in Cooley's classic phrase, are "looking-glass selves." We have no other way of discovering who and what we are than from the reflections that come from others' words and actions. A child who continually sees in the "mirrors" around him, "You are inferior, you are bad, you are incompetent," will internalize those attitudes toward himself. Only a powerful contradicting image from a loving mother, a teacher, a friend, or a successful person from his group with whom he has identified can furnish the basis for self-respect.

Many Indians did become cruel, lacking in ambition, untrustworthy. Many Negroes are lazy, uneducated, irresponsible. It is not uncommon for the members of a minority group to learn some degree of self-hatred, to lack motivation, to feel less than fully attached to the norms of a society that treats them unfairly. Thus a system of discrimination that starts out by rationalizing its own actions by selective perception and stereotypy, ends by creating its own justification. This is one of the most important illustrations of the self-fulfilling prophecy, or in less neutral terms the vicious circle.[17] If I say, "It's going to rain tomorrow," my prophecy has nothing to do with the actual course of events. But if I say: "I'm going to flunk that exam tomorrow," the statement may become involved in a process of rationalization and activity—why should I study? I won't pass anyway; why should I study? the movie is awfully interesting; why did I fall so far behind? I can't sleep from worrying—that helps to bring about the very event that was prophesied. Such a cycle is a significant part of minority-majority situations. The result is that the prejudices of the majority have continual reenforcement, which deepens them and helps to justify further discrimination, which in turn gives further reenforcement to the tendencies of minorities.

Put in this way, the vicious circle seems to be perpetual and unbreachable. Were this literally true, we would have to affirm that "Once a minority, always a minority." Worse than that, it would appear that the level of discrimination would continually rise. There is firm evidence, however, that this is not true. To return to our example of American Indians, it is clear that other Americans hold a less stereotyped picture of them today, discriminate less against them, and are more ready to accept either assimilation or pluralism than has been true in the past. We shall show in some detail in Chapter 5 that discrimination against Negroes is on the decline. The vicious circle of minority-majority relations, then, should be seen as a sociological law that operates under certain stated conditions. The student of society tries to discover those conditions and also the circumstances that promote an upward spiral. We will discuss those circumstances later, but meanwhile we must be thoroughly aware that a pattern of discrimination is a very firm structure, with several mutually reenforcing supports. Only powerful forces, skillfully used, can bring it down.

NEGROES
IN THE UNITED STATES:

segregation becomes a social problem

Up until now we have been concerned with general principles and definitions related to minority groups. To give these substance, we must examine particular situations with full attention to the patterns of majority-minority relations in them and the direction of change. Almost anywhere we look in the modern world there are examples deserving careful examination. Because the evidence is full and the pressures both for change and for stability are great—sharply revealing the causal forces at work—we shall use the status of American Negroes as our case study. As you do your own further study of minority groups, you will want to bring to bear on other situations the kind of evidence we report here for one group; for only on the basis of a full command of the facts can we arrive at accurate interpretations and responsible moral judgments.

The first thing that strikes one as he begins a study of the status of American Negroes in the mid-1960s is the powerful momentum for change. We have heard such terms as revolution and explosion so often in recent years that they have lost their dramatic value; but this should not cause us to forget that this *is* a period of dramatic change—not least of all in the nature of intergroup contact. There are patterns of racial and cultural relations in the United States that were difficult to imagine twenty-five years ago. Although not without exception, the strongest trends have been in the direction of greater integration. Let us document that fact carefully, examine some of the forces producing it and opposing it, and explore its significance for American society.

The term integration is used in various ways. In referring to an integrated society, I shall have in mind one in which the members, regardless of race, religion, or national origin, move freely among one another, sharing the same opportunities and the same public facilities and privileges on an equal basis. Does the term imply also the absence of any barriers to purely private associations? Yes, if one is thinking of *full* integration; for we are dealing with a variable that can have many different scale values.

Whereas integration is a state of affairs, desegregation is a process. It is a process of change within a society during which the degree of segregation is reduced. This too is a variable; desegregation can range from a small increase in the amount of interaction across group lines—as when three or four Negro children are admitted to a formerly all-white school—to a major reduction in the number and height of the barriers to association. In this sense, it is not entirely meaningful to say that a factory or school or church has been "de-segregated"—as if one were speaking of an either-or situation. We shall occasionally, however, for the sake of convenience, use that term to mean that a formerly fully segregated situation has taken one or more steps toward integration. In most instances the first step is the most difficult and critical, which partly justifies referring to it as desegregation.

Segregation Becomes a Social Problem

It is important to ask how the process of desegregation is set in motion, sometimes breaking up stable patterns of segregation that have existed for many generations. There are varieties of segregation in all societies. To some degree it is the natural expression of group identity and function. Few persons object if chemists are barred from the American Economic Association or persons of Anglo-Saxon descent are ineligible for membership in the Polish-American Club. Some forms of segregation are repugnant to a society, however, because they violate its basic values or because they create enormous problems. In fact, the word segregation often implies exclusion on grounds that are irrelevant to the putative functions or aims of a group. We shall often use the term in this narrower sense.

Conflict over segregation may occur because the lines of separation that are taken for granted or approved in a society do not remain static. As a result of social change which creates new issues for the nation to handle, forms of segregation become unacceptable that formerly were allowed. But since the change hits individuals and regions in different ways and at different rates, there is often a period of sharp controversy during which some persons say: The old way represents a desirable pluralism and a legitimate separation, while others say: The old way represents a threat to the health of the society. Thus segregation fits our definition of a social problem most exactly.

A century ago, women in the United States were a minority group, subject to discriminatory treatment, as they still are to some degree. Gradually, however, owing to the way our society was developing, discriminatory treatment of women became an unhappy fact for a few, then objectionable to many, and finally repugnant to most. Legal and customary norms changed to formalize a new status for women.

The United States is now in the midst of a similar process with respect to racial and religious segregation. Segregation is no longer simply taken for granted; the older patterns of intergroup relations are rapidly being modified. Before examining the evidence for that statement, let me state briefly why segregation has become a social problem—a subject for public concern and debate—rather than being quietly accepted by most persons as natural or desirable, as it had been for decades. To answer this question fully would require a careful examination of the changes in American society; but a brief statement may suggest some of the forces at work:

Societies express a "strain toward consistency"—a tendency to reduce obvious discrepancies among their major value patterns and institutional structures. This tendency may be blocked by other forces; it may express itself strongly or weakly, depending upon the situation; but it should not be disregarded. As applied to segregation, the strain toward consistency is a force tending to bring the patterns of race relations into harmony with the basic values and processes of the economic, political, and religious institutions. Among these are individual freedom, equality before the law, and the sanctity of the person.

Segregation in the United States had its origin in a plantation society. In a sense it "fit" with that kind of society—that is, it could exist within the society without seriously disrupting its operations. But segregation is a hindrance to the smooth functioning of urban, mobile, industrial, democratic societies. The premium such societies place upon such values as individualism, judgment by merit, and the maximum development of talent requires the development of "universalistic" criteria of judgment—the placement of individuals according to their capabilities, not according to their group membership. This principle has great relevance for any society undergoing rapid change. It applies, for example, to South Africa, where apartheid, a relentless policy of segregation, is proclaimed as the official way. But South Africa is trying also to continue to develop a modern, industrial economic system. This requires a skilled, literate, mobile, and well-motivated labor force, most of which will have to be recruited from the nonwhite population, since persons of European descent make up less than one-quarter of the population. I think it is correct to say that South Africa can have apartheid or it can have a modern economy, but it cannot have both.[1] It is highly problematic whether the ruling groups will discover this choice soon enough to prevent utter tragedy there.

Without attempting to discuss all the reasons why segregation has become a social problem in the United States, let me mention two additional influences: The vast increase in communication and interaction among nations has meant that America's deviations from her democratic creed seriously affect her position of leadership among the free nations; and segregated and disprivileged groups have gained a great deal of power in the last generation, power with which to fight much more effectively than in the past for equality of opportunity. The increases in education, in income, in political participation, and in the effectiveness of their protest organizations make Negro Americans and other minorities better able to attack the walls of segregation.

Thus there are powerful forces supporting the desegregation process. To understand contemporary developments and the probable course of future events, we must be careful not to make our judgments on the basis of the headlines, which often call attention to disagreement and conflict. Flowing beneath the surface ripples there are often deeper currents moving in a different direction. Conflict, in fact, may only show that the old order is being pressed. Those who approved it and had taken it for granted now find themselves obliged to try to defend it. We will be wise also to remember that desegregation is a national, not simply a Southern, question. Virtually all of the persons of Puerto Rican descent, many of the Mexican-Americans, and half of the Negroes in the United States now live in the North and West. The national aspect of the process is shown particularly clearly in political developments. With more than three million registered Negro voters in the North and West and nearly two million in the South and with many more to come, both Democrats and Republicans show increasing interest in their problems. In 1957, 1960, and 1964, they united to pass the first civil rights bills to come out of Congress in three-quarters of a century—bills that will feed on their own successes as they reduce the barriers to further participation in politics by Negroes.

The economy is also national in scope. This fact was little understood by Arkansas businessmen in 1957, when many of them stood aside or supported Governor Faubus in his attempts to prevent the integration of Central High School in Little Rock. The result was a sharp reduction in the rate of industrial growth in the city. After averaging five major new plants a year from 1950 to 1957, Little Rock added not a single major plant in the next four years.[2] Dallas, Richmond, and Atlanta businessmen were quick to learn the significance of this. They have been among the leaders in the slow but peaceful beginnings of desegregation in those cities.

The process of desegregation demonstrates clearly the interdependence of the institutions as well as the regions of a society. Changes in the school system affect, and are affected by, changes in the economy, political patterns, international relations, religious practices, and other aspects of the life of a society. Because of the mutual influence of the parts of a society, we are not free to support segregation or integration simply as a matter of taste. As a society becomes more urban and industrial, and particularly if these developments take place in a democratic context, segregation becomes more and more difficult to maintain.

These principles are well supported by what has happened in the United States during the last twenty-five years. For two generations after the Civil War, segregation was taken for granted by almost everyone. There were changes during this period, but the pace was so slow that even the cumulative effect over several decades was slight. Then, beginning perhaps in the early 1930s, there was a quickening in the rate of change. In Ralph McGill's telling phrase, "Desegregation began with the boll weevil." This little beetle probably began to chew away at the cotton economy before 1920, but in the 1930s he was helped by a depression which undermined the one-crop economy, by federal attention to crop diversification, and by the increased rate of urbanization and industrialization in the South.

Paradoxically, many an ardent segregationist was also a supporter of the efforts to bring industry into the South, often without realizing that he was making a fundamental choice. Urbanization, the increase in industrial jobs with hourly pay rates, the beginnings of unionization, diversification of jobs for Negroes, the growth in literacy and awareness of democratic values, the sharp increase in the size of the urban middle class, a growing integration of the national economy—these and other forces are changing the patterns of race relations in all parts of the country.[3]

Although it started from a lower base, the South has been industrializing and urbanizing more rapidly than the rest of the nation for the last twenty-five years. Among other things, this has meant a tremendous migration of Negroes away from the rural areas, most of them to Northern cities. In the 1940s, 1,245,000 nonwhites, almost all of them Negroes, migrated to the North and West. In the 1950s migration was even heavier: 1,457,000 non-whites, one out of seven of those living in the South in 1950, moved out of the region. At the same time, the colored population of Southern cities has been increasing at a rapid rate, a fact of great significance in understanding the process of desegregation.

The Negro sharecropper and tenant, with his vast dependence upon the plantation owner in almost every aspect of life, is being replaced by the town worker. His work is still largely on the unskilled level and his income is low; but there are important differences. Hourly pay rates, an increasing need for semi-skilled and skilled workers, public welfare services, increased shopping in town stores tend to bring Negroes into the more impersonal "market" of the city. The merchant and the industrialist are caught in much sharper cross-pressures than the plantation owner. The merchant may believe in segregation, but he also believes in cus-tomers. The industrialist, interested in the rational organization of pro-duction, is not happy with artificial restraints on his use of the labor force.[4]

Opposition to Desegregation

It would be a mistake, of course, to overlook the vigor and effective-ness of opposition to desegregation. Desegregation is a social problem in both meanings of the term—that is, there are disagreements over both means and ends—and the type of opposition to it is influenced by this distinction. Those who "know" that segregation is good and integration evil are ready to go to very great lengths to prevent Negro children from entering a "white" school, to block Negro adults from registering to vote, or to deny Negro families the opportunity of buying or renting a house in an all-white neighbor-hood. Opposition for some does not stop at murder, and in the last few years more than a dozen persons have been killed. Perhaps the most poignant example is the murder of four little Negro girls in Birmingham, Alabama, in 1963. While they were attending Sunday school, a bomb was thrown into their church, killing them and injuring twenty others. To cite another case of violence, when a Federal court ordered the admission of a Negro to "their" school, students at the University of Mississippi, and many outsiders who joined them, rioted in protest, attacking the Federal marshals responsible for enforcing the order, burning cars, demanding the new student's removal. During the conflict, two persons were killed.

Some persons who share the view that segregation is good are not ready to go to such lengths themselves; but they may give support and encouragement to mobs, whether by intent or ignorance, by encouraging the view that Federal intervention is unconstitutional and inviting disregard of the law. Governor Wallace of Alabama, for example, deplored the bombing in Birmingham; but the *News and Observer* of Raleigh, North Carolina, observed: "Certainly Alabama Governor George C. Wallace's description of the bombing as 'a tragic event which has saddened the hearts of all Alabamians' has a tragically hollow ring. Every action he has taken since he became Governor has been designed to encourage blind resistance to change, to loose the furies of racial prejudice and hatred." There have been over fifty bombings of Negro buildings and homes in Birmingham since World War II, and not one of these crimes has been solved.[5]

Not all opposition entails violence. In some communities, officials have closed schools rather than to permit them to operate on an integrated basis. Resistance to the registration of Negroes for voting takes many forms, from unequal application of registration procedures, to intimidation and economic reprisal.[6] Whites as well as Negroes are affected by the opposition; in those areas where most of the power is in the hands of persons dedicated to segregation, moderate or liberal white persons who support desegregation are threatened, boycotted, or removed from positions of influence in many cases. The *New York Times* has reported from Mississippi, for example:

A move to purge Mississippi of white leaders who disagree with the state's rigid segregation policies has met with increasing success in recent months.

The move, spearheaded by the white Citizens Councils, has been under way for several years. It has shown marked acceleration since the University of Mississippi riots last year.

Many white leaders have left the state, either under pressure or because they did not feel they could be effective under existing conditions.

Others, while remaining in the state, have been removed from sensitive positions or have stepped down voluntarily after encountering hostility.

The move has been most evident in the fields of politics, education and religion. The result has been a general lessening of opposition to massive resistance to integration, both in the public and private sectors.[7]

In a sociological study of social problems it is always of great interest to ask: Who takes what side in the value conflict, and how is the position of each related to his place in society? Many studies have documented the circumstances related to opposition to desegregation: Those areas where the level of education is lowest, the economy in deepest trouble, the population declining, the proportion of Negroes highest, the tradition of violence strongest, and the range of political debate and political alternatives narrowest, among many other variables, are the areas where resistance is strongest. These conditions are not mutually exclusive and not all apply to each situation where the opposition is powerful; but they guide us to settings of probable conflict.[8]

Leaders of and participants in mobs are generally poorly educated and economically insecure. This may lead one to conclude, too readily, that they oppose integration while the better educated and more prosperous are willing to accept it. This is partly true; but it is also partly true that the difference is more a matter of method than of goal. Campbell notes that the urban middle class did not participate in the violent opposition to desegregation of Central High School in Little Rock; but they had built a new high school for their children on the edge of the city where problems of integration were least likely to arise. Thus the "moderate" urban middle-class group, since they understood community processes and controlled the mechanisms of decision, "had no need to resort to violence; they had alternative methods of securing their ends."[9]

Segregation as a social problem is by no means limited to the South. This point needs to be made without exaggerating it, for there is certainly more support for integration in the North and West. There are fewer institutional areas where segregation is an issue; barriers to voting and to use of public facilities, for example, are high only in the South; and opposition to segregation is more likely to be based on the means and the speed of change than on its direction. A critically important difference is the fact that, outside of the South, most influential leaders and most official norms and laws support desegregation. Compile a list of statements from college presidents, governors, trade union officials, and local clergymen, for example, from Mississippi and New York, and the difference will be sharp.

Nevertheless, in the North and West, desegregation is far from a simply technical problem; that is, it is not only a matter of finding the best means for accomplishing an agreed-upon goal; there are values in conflict—the heart of a social problem. The focus of the problem is upon housing, jobs, and schools, three closely related and interdependent issues. Millions of families in the last decade have struggled painfully to get out of the deteriorating areas of our large cities. They may have bought their first house, in a modest but respectable part of the city, or they may have moved to the suburbs to find a little grass and a better school for their children. Thus they have won a little of that social honor so important in a stratification system; but they have won only a little, and they are not certain how secure it is. They are not willingly going to endanger it by permitting their neighborhoods to be desegregated. It requires a great deal of optimism to expect them to be social philosophers concerned with the costs of segregation to minority-group members and to the whole society. (We will note later that to change the actions of such people, one must pay attention to the structural conditions—the sources of insecurity and misinformation—more than to their attitudes, which are largely a result of those conditions.)

Some of the resisting whites might not be unhappy if 5, or 10 or even 20 percent of their neighbors were colored, but they have seen whole neighborhoods "turn over" in a few years (granted the particular economic, housing, and demographic conditions of mid-twentieth century in the United States, this is not an uncommon occurrence), and they generalize this into a universal and inevitable principle. Their own predictions then become part of a self-fulfilling prophecy, because on the basis of their predictions of what must inevitably take place, they sell in panic—encouraged by agents who are well rewarded by neighborhood changes—thus bringing about the very outcome they fear. This is a highly complicated question which we will discuss more fully later; but it is, and seems likely to remain for some years ahead, the most difficult aspect of desegregation in the North and West.

Opposition to racial integration of jobs is in part a manifestation of a common desire by those in an occupation to keep tight control over job opportunities. The American Medical Association disagrees sharply with those who believe that there should be a large increase in the number of physicians. There are serious obstacles to training for many skilled crafts, even those in which there are shortages of workers. These obstacles are a manifestation of the desire for gain on one side and the fear, however remote, of loss of job on the other. Economic reasons for opposition to desegregation loom large also for those in jobs in which unemployment is common and automation is a serious threat. As students of social problems we will be wise to keep in mind the ways in which a person's location in society —his status, the degree of security of that status, the outlook on the world of the groups with which he identifies, and the hopes or threats that life seems to offer—influences his actions toward minority groups. Opposition to desegregation is not so much a personal idiosyncrasy as it is a demonstration of stresses and strains in society. It is these which require particular attention.

DESEGREGATION:

changes in minority-group status

Such facts as those examined in the preceding chapter are indicative of serious resistance to the development of a racially integrated society. No student of minority groups can afford to overlook or to minimize them. More important for those seeking to understand the contemporary scene, however, are the evidences of change. It is scarcely surprising that strong forces seek to preserve an established institutional pattern. It is more noteworthy that extensive change is under way. Desegregation has begun, not simply in one or two institutions, but in almost every aspect of national life. In the next few pages I shall try to document that statement sufficiently to permit us to judge the extent to which the United States is becoming an integrated society.

Judicial and Legal Changes

Among the most influential forces for desegregation have been Supreme Court decisions and local, state, and Federal laws which together have severely narrowed the legal bases for segregation. Without attempting a complete catalog, I can indicate the scope of the legal change by listing several of the Court decisions and laws. In 1915, the Supreme Court declared that "grandfather clauses" in state constitutions or statutes, patently designed to prevent Negroes from voting, were unconstitutional. In 1917, laws that required housing segregation were prohibited; and in 1948, the Court ruled that private "restrictive covenants" designed to preserve segregated areas could not be upheld in the courts. One of the major decisions was handed down in 1944, when the "white primary"— the basic device for the disfranchisement of Negroes—was forbidden by the Supreme Court. Beginning in 1938 and reaching a climax in 1954, with its decision outlawing segregation in all public education, the Supreme Court set in motion the process of school desegregation. In 1946, segregation in interstate travel was banned; and in 1955, the Court ruled against segregation in public recreational facilities. In 1963, the constitution was amended to forbid a poll tax as a voting requirement in Federal elections.

Such decisions as these did not, of course, immediately transform the practices against which they were directed. I will cite below some of the evidence concerning the extent of compliance. What the Supreme Court decisions do represent is a major transformation of the *Plessy v. Ferguson* doctrine (1896) which established the principle of "separate but equal" as legally acceptable. That Court decision can be thought of as the judicial equivalent of the political "compromise of 1876." It represented a period of indifference on the part of the Supreme Court to laws and practices of segregation and discrimination, because in practice, during the next forty years, segregation meant "separate and unequal." That indifference began to disappear, however, in the 1930s, and twenty years later it was gone entirely. Reversal of the *Plessy v. Ferguson* decision came in two stages. At first the Court became more and more insistent that if facilities were separate they must at least be equal. But in the school decision of 1954, a significant second stage was reached: Segregated facilities were declared to be inherently unequal.

Of the scores of local, state, and Federal laws supporting the process of desegregation, the following are perhaps the most important: Twenty-one states, beginning with New York in 1945, and over forty cities, had passed fair employment practices laws by 1963. These laws vary widely in scope and in the powers granted to enforcement commissions, but their total effect has been to increase significantly the employment opportunities of minority-group workers. Sixty percent of the population of the country, including nearly half of the minority-group population, resides in states and cities covered by these laws. Since 1950, sixteen states and many cities have passed fair housing practices laws. All of the statutes refer to publicly assisted housing—which now includes a high proportion of the houses being built—and eleven cover at least some of the private housing market. In addition New York, Pittsburgh, and other cities bar discrimination in much of their privately financed housing. On the Federal level, the Civil Rights bills of 1957, 1960, and 1964, concerned primarily with voting rights, public accommodations, and economic opportunity, were the first civil rights bills passed by Congress since 1875.

Thus the United States has taken many decisive judicial and legal steps to reduce the disprivileges of minority-group members.

Politics

These judicial and legal developments can be partly understood as a result of changes in the United States affecting the political power of minority groups, especially of Negroes, who constitute over 10 percent of the population. Three factors are of greatest importance in these changes: The elimination of the white primary, in 1944, has been followed by a steady increase in Negro registration and voting in the South. In 1944, there were approximately 250,000 registered Negro voters in the South; in 1964 there were over seven times that many. It should be noted, however, that this still represents only about 30 percent of the potential Negro electorate in the South, compared with a registration of 60 percent among Southern whites. In the North and West, there are over 3 million registered Negro voters. Inevitably the increased voting power of Negroes has resulted in competition for their support in areas where there are many Negro voters. Negroes in such districts have won better police protection, more attention to their school needs, and an abatement of racist campaigns. Many have been elected to public office on the local level.

The second cause of the change has been the growth in size and importance of the white, urban middle class in the South. Their political interests do not all coincide with those of the landed gentry. Intra- and interparty competition is developing. And where parties and politicians compete, they seek votes from formerly neglected groups. Urban voters are grossly underrepresented in American politics, particularly on the state level, and particularly in the South. In recent years they have begun to see that they are not well served by a tightly controlled, oligarchic political pattern, an important part of which is disfranchisement of Negroes. Party competition is still very slight in many parts of the South, as it is in some other parts of the nation. But the pattern is changing along with the residential and economic patterns of the region. It is too early to judge the effects of the Supreme Court decisions in 1964, making equal representation mandatory in Federal elections and state legislatures, but they seem likely to change the composition of Congress and legislatures in ways that will be significant for race relations. The Negro voter will become more important, and the more discriminatory white voters will become less important as the requirement is carried out.

The third force affecting the political role of minorities in the United States has been the vast migratory movement of Negroes to Northern cities. In at least eight industrial states, colored voters now hold strategic "balance of power" positions. To neglect their interests is to court political defeat.

The effect of these three developments, supported by the increase in the educational level and economic power of minorities, has been to give strong political impetus to the desegregation process. To illustrate the growth in political power among colored voters: In 1956, at least three of the five Southern states won by President Eisenhower were carried by Negro votes, in the sense that the *increase* in Negro votes over his 1952 total was larger than his margin of victory. The President won Tennessee by five thousand votes; but in

Memphis alone the net Negro shift to the Republican ticket was twenty thousand. In 1956, of course, the final outcome in the nation was not affected by these shifts. This was not the case, however, in 1960. The average shift from the Republican to the Democratic ticket between 1956 and 1960 was 8 percent, just barely enough to elect President Kennedy. Among Negro voters, there was a shift of 16 percent. Had the Democrats increased their vote among Negroes by only the 8 percent that was the national average, Mr. Nixon would have been elected President. President Kennedy's margin of victory in Texas, South Carolina, Illinois, New Jersey, Michigan, and several other states was far smaller than the number of votes he received from Negroes. These simple facts have not been overlooked by either party and will surely affect future campaigns.

The Armed Forces

Closely related to the legal and political changes that we have discussed has been the desegregation of the Armed Forces of the United States since 1950. With only minor exceptions, all branches of the service segregated colored from white troops before and during the Second World War. In the period of the "gathering storm," to use Winston Churchill's phrase to refer to American race relations rather than to the world scene, the discriminatory treatment of Negro servicemen was a critical fact, giving momentum and direction to the protest movement that was beginning. As James Baldwin has said regarding the earlier situation:

The treatment accorded the Negro during the Second World War marks, for me, a turning point in the Negro's relation to America. To put it briefly, and somewhat too simply, a certain hope died, a certan respect for white Americans faded. One began to pity them, or to hate them. You must put yourself in the skin of a man who is wearing the uniform of his country, is a candidate for death in its defense, and who is called a "nigger" by his comrades-in-arms and his officers; who is almost always given the hardest, ugliest, most menial work to do; who knows that the white G.I. has informed the Europeans that he is subhuman (so much for the American male's sexual security); who does not dance at the U.S.O. the night white soldiers dance there, and does not drink in the same bars white soldiers drink in; and who watches German prisoners of war being treated by Americans with more human dignity than he has ever received at their hands.[1]

One does not need to take this statement as the full truth—it does in fact leave out much contrary evidence and is filled with its own stereotypy—to realize the significance of the feelings it represents. More than a million Negro servicemen returned home after World War II both less willing to accept discrimination and better prepared, by attitude and skill, to fight it. This makes particularly important the abrupt change in the policy of segregation in the Armed Forces. After receiving the report of his Committee on Equality of Treatment and Opportunity in the Armed Services in 1950, President Truman ordered an immediate and rapid integration of all branches of the service. By 1954, the *New York Times* wrote, perhaps only slightly prematurely, that racial integration in the Armed Forces is "one of the biggest stories of the twentieth century." In a period of three or four years, most of the barriers to the participation of colored Americans had been removed.

In 1962, Negro participation, by percentage, in the four branches of the service was as follows:[2]

	Army	Air Force	Navy	Marine Corps
Officer	3.2	1.2	0.3	0.2
Warrant officer	3.3	1.2	0.3	0.3
Enlisted	12.2	9.2	5.2	7.6
Total	11.1	7.8	4.7	7.0

Judged against the 10.5 percent which Negroes make up of the total population, it is clear that they are still vastly underrepresented in the officer corps, particularly of the Navy and the Marine Corps. This fact is partly indicative, however, especially in the Army and Air Force, of a lack of seniority and of training. Only to a residual degree does it represent a lack of equal treatment. With only thirty-six Negroes in the three military academies in 1963, their underrepresentation there is perhaps more serious, as is the failure of the Navy and the Marine Corps to employ Negroes in technical jobs, electronics, automobile mechanics, and the like, in a proportion even as large as is found in the civilian economy.

Integration of the Armed Forces has been accompanied by integration of government-owned shore installations and other facilities for civilian employees and of schools for the children of servicemen. It has also meant that more Negroes are getting skilled training, some are receiving increased income, and throughout the services there has been an increase of equal-status contact across race lines.

Employment and Income

In this brief listing I can only illustrate the changes affecting minority-group families that are taking place in the American economic system. Particularly since 1940, colored workers have made substantial gains in the income and skill levels of their jobs. Not all of the gains have been accompanied by desegregation, but the tendency is for the walls of separation to be lowered along with the lowering of differentials in income and skill.

In the last generation, homeownership has increased half again as rapidly among nonwhites as among whites. The increase in the proportions finishing high school and college has been twice as great for colored as it has been for white persons. The increase among the former, of course, has been built on a lower base. The average income of nonwhite families in 1930 was approximately 30 percent of the average for white families. For the next twenty-five years the average income of nonwhite families went up at an average rate of 1 percent per year, so that by the mid-1950s, it stood at about 55 percent of that of white families. At this point the rate of growth of the American economy began to fall off, and unemployment began to grow. Recessions in 1958 and 1961 seriously lowered the income of those families least able to endure a decline. The result was that the formerly steady improvement in the ratio of Negro to white income stopped. By 1963—a year of dramatic protests—it still remained at about 55 percent. There can be no doubt that, in the immediate situation, reduction of the economic disprivilege of Negroes has been seriously slowed.

From a longer-range point of view, perhaps the most important

aspect of the economic situation is the changing job pattern. Although still seriously disprivileged, the colored population has made
important gains in the stable core of urban jobs for men—doubtless
the best index of its place in the American economy. On the white-
collar level, which includes professional, managerial, clerical, and
sales jobs, the percentage of white male workers increased, between
1940 and 1962, from 30.3 to 41.2 percent, while the percentage of
nonwhite male workers in these jobs increased from 5.6 to 16.0 percent. Although the latter change is slightly smaller in *absolute*
amount (10.4 to 10.9 percent), the *relative* gain for the nonwhites is much larger. On the semiskilled and skilled job levels,
colored men made steady gains during the same period. The
increase among white workers was from 34.3 to 38.6 percent; among
nonwhites it was from 16.6 to 32.7 percent. Most of these workers
were recruited from the ranks of the unskilled and from among farm
laborers, hence the new jobs represented significant improvement
in their economic status.[3]

It should not be forgotten that colored workers have constantly
been hit more severely than whites by unemployment, at a ratio of
more than 2 to 1. Because their jobs are more often on the lower
levels of skill, nonwhites are more seriously affected by automation.
Without a major effort to upgrade education and skill, this burden
will continue to be heavy. Many forces, however, support the trend
toward improvement in their occupational situation. Without dis-
cussing their various contributions, I would mention urban migration,
improved education, labor unions, state and local fair employment
practices laws, Federal civil service and contract policy, the work of
the President's Committee on Equal Employment Opportunity, and,
perhaps most important, the high level of economic prosperity in
the nation as the forces most significantly sustaining the gains among
minority-group workers. Some of these forces have had ambivalent
results, to be sure, but their net effect has been to increase the
desegregation of the economy of the United States. There is some
evidence that the dramatic protest movement of the 1960s has
helped to crack many job barriers in the skilled crafts, in business,
and in government employment. It is too early to tell how many

Negroes will benefit from these changes, but there is good reason to believe that there may be a climb up from the plateau of 1955 to 1963.[4]

Housing

The extensive migratory movement of colored families into the cities of the nation and the improvement of their incomes, among other elements, have focused increasing attention on residential segregation. In many ways this is more a Northern than a Southern question, for the most numerous blocks of segregated houses are in the large Northern cities. Many Yankees who criticize the South for its segregated schools defend housing arrangements that have many of the same consequences for race relations and for personality development that school segregation has.

Housing desegregation has proceeded more slowly than almost any other phase of the process of change. Most contractors and developers build for white families only; a few build only for colored families; and a tiny fraction—a few score throughout the nation—build integrated projects. There are many integrated public housing units; yet there is a tendency among some of these to drift toward segregation. Even the process of urban redevelopment sometimes increases segregation: the deteriorated housing, often occupied by minority-group families, may be replaced by units too expensive for them to afford. They are forced into the already overcrowded segregated areas, which contributes further to their deterioration.

Some persons who accept integration in public facilities or in jobs resist the idea of desegregating housing because it represents a change near the social end of the scale of contact. A family's status is strongly influenced by its housing situation. This is complicated by the fact that a house represents a major lifetime expenditure. Housing costs are high, and for many years housing has been in short supply in most parts of the United States. The increase of the nonwhite population of the cities has been far more rapid than the increase in housing available to them—with resulting pressure and tension. In such a setting, powerful interests are able to profit by the sale of exclusiveness on one hand and by overcrowding on the other.

The Commission on Race and Housing has estimated that one-sixth of the American people are to some degree restricted in their choice of residence. Many of them, as a result, are forced into slums. These areas mean to their residents not only overcrowding and dilapidated housing; they mean scarcity of parks, poor sanitation facilities, the mixture of commerce and industry into the residential area, and the prevalence of crime and vice.[5] It should be said that living conditions for minority groups in the United States have probably improved in the last several decades. But our national income and our national standards for minimum housing have also gone up, increasing the gap between what we have and what we accept as a national goal and policy.

The consequences of residential segregation are severe, both for those who experience it and for the total community. Housing segregation usually leads to other forms of segregation—in schools, parks, churches, hospitals, and public accommodations. It is often associated with discrimination in such forms as poorer police and fire protection, lower standards of sanitation, dilapidated schools, and lax enforcement of housing codes. Their lack of choice in housing makes colored Americans vulnerable to rental and purchase prices up to 40 percent higher than white Americans pay for equivalent accommodations—a heavy overcharge for those who are least able to pay. Many slum residents are recent migrants to the city. They have a great deal to learn about how to live in a city, but their isolation blocks them from the pressures to learn. The group is turned in upon itself, developing its own code of behavior in a context of frustration and hopelessness. The motivations and self-conceptions of segregated children are negatively influenced by a setting of subcultures and contracultures that separate them from others in their city.

It is not only the minority-group member who suffers from this situation. The total community loses potential skills. Residential segregation creates conditions within which hostility and antisocial behavior can develop. It promotes the growth of slums, with a variety of negative effects on a community; and when the slums are cleared, the displaced population, often unable to afford the new housing, piles up in other areas, making new slums. Segregation also creates problems in the foreign relations of the United States. And by increasing distant and stereotype-laden contact, it promotes prejudices that tear the fabric of community life.[6]

We would be wise to remember that the United States, indeed the world, is on a one-way street leading toward urbanism of one kind or another. So far, the process has gone on largely unguided, and even unstudied, except by a few specialists. Americans may prefer to turn their backs on this process, but it will not stop and its consequences will not be avoided. No aspect of this trend toward a totally urban civilization is more important than the present haphazard absorption into our metropolitan areas of groups with vastly differing opportunities and of various subcultures, yet who are in vitally close communication and interdependence.

Although segregation in housing is overwhelmingly common, a close look will reveal even in this aspect of national life increasingly important tendencies toward desegregation. A new trend began—insofar as one can give a date to such a social process—about 1950, and in the last five years it has shown a significant increase in strength. At first, the Federal Housing Authority and other governmental agencies concerned with housing considered segregated housing both natural and desirable. In the last decade, however, they have increasingly allowed and encouraged the development of integrated projects. In November, 1962, President Kennedy issued a long-awaited administrative order requiring that all new governmentally assisted housing be rented or sold without regard to race, religion, or national origin. This was a less sweeping decision than many persons expected and believed mandatory. Colored Americans are now being taxed, along with others, to support various housing programs in whose benefits they are not equally entitled to share. At least since the Boston Tea Party, this kind of situation has been unacceptable in America and it is, without doubt, unconstitutional.

We noted above that state and local laws, as well as Federal actions, are beginning to restrict housing segregation. These laws are based not only on the constitutional grounds of due process (the illegality of being taxed without sharing equally in the benefits), but also on the police power of the community (the right to protect itself against blight and the unhappy consequences of residential deterioration). The statutes of the sixteen states and numerous communities that seek to reduce housing discrimination have, wherever they have enforcement powers, generated opposition. Inevitably such laws restrict the freedom of landlords, just as most laws restrict freedom in some measure. The question is: Do the laws contribute to the welfare of the total community and to the freedom of the presently segregated groups? In my judgment they do; and I believe that in the long run they will place very few restraints on the freedom of most landlords. Indeed, those who own and rent houses will profit greatly by the general community gains from housing desegregation. Those few who now gain from the restricted choices of nonwhites and from the resulting overcrowding would, as a result of desegregation, find slum housing less profitable.

I can list only a few of the other forces that are beginning to support the desegregation of housing. Some labor unions, with interracial membership, are entering the mortgage market. There is evidence pointing to a general reduction in prejudice and a slight shift in attitudes toward integrated residential areas, perhaps based on the growing acquaintance with the favorable responses of those who live in such areas. A few score private builders are now explicitly developing interracial districts.[7] And a large number of churches have circulated open-occupancy covenants. These are the reverse of the restrictive covenants that extralegally, but not yet illegally, segregate so many American neighborhoods along racial and religious lines. Thousands of church members have signed pledges similar to this: "I will welcome into my neighborhood as a resident any person of good character, regardless of race, religion, or national origin." Thus they seek to weaken the assertion that segregation persists only because residents will not accept integrated neighborhoods.

During the last twenty years, residential segregation has probably increased in the United States. This is certainly true in the large Northern cities. Now, however, important pressures to reverse this trend have developed. Since they are very recent, their impact cannot easily be measured, but supported as they are by other pressures toward desegregation, it seems likely that they will grow in strength and that housing desegregation will proceed at an increasingly rapid pace.

Education

No aspect of the process of desegregation has received more attention than the changes in American schools. It is scarcely necessary to mention the strategic importance of education, both to individuals and to the whole group, in a society based on democratic political forms and diverse occupational skills. Those who are blocked from educational advance are kept in low status even if other influences favor their development. A group that is given educational opportunities has a powerful instrument with which to improve its status, even if for the moment other influences are unfavorable. In America, education has been one of the most important ladders up which disprivileged persons have climbed to better positions. Certainly the extent, if not always the quality, of our educational opportunities is an exciting and important part of the American resolve to maintain an open society.

The long-run trend has been to make the educational ladder available to more and more groups in the United States. Desegregation is only the most recent manifestation of this trend. I shall not review here the series of court decisions and the voluntary changes that have, since the late 1930s, slowly expanded the educational opportunities of colored Americans and reduced the barriers of segregation. An important turning point was reached in 1954 when the Supreme Court ruled that any segregation in public schools was unconstitutional. This was followed in 1955 by an order that all school districts must proceed to integrate their schools "with all deliberate speed," for the Court recognized that there would be difficult problems to solve.

At the time of the 1954 decision, all of the schools in the Southern region, which is composed of seventeen states plus the District of Columbia, were segregated. As of 1964, over 42 percent of the biracial school districts (1,289 of 3,026) have been desegregated to some degree. More than four out of five acted voluntarily. In some instances, as in Washington, D.C., integration is complete; in others, the change has been the barest minimum. The states can be classified into four groups. First are the border states, where extensive integration has taken place: 56 percent of the Negro children go to school with white children; and over 90 percent of the biracial school districts have been desegregated: West Virginia, Delaware, Missouri, Kentucky, Maryland, Oklahoma, and Washington, D.C. Four states (Texas, Tennessee, Virginia, and Florida) have had slight desegregation, involving one-third of their school districts and from 2 percent to 5 percent of their Negro children. There has been token integration in seven states, ranging from sixty students in Mississippi to over three thousand in North Carolina, with South Carolina, Alabama, Georgia, Arkansas, and Louisiana in between. In each case less than 1 percent of the Negro pupils attend integrated schools. In total, 9.3 percent of the Negro children in the Southern region now go to school with white children, nine-tenths of these in the border area. Teacher integration is extensive in the border states and Washington, D.C., and has begun in Florida, Tennessee, Texas, and Virginia.[8]

Desegregation of graduate schools and colleges began even before the 1954 Supreme Court decision and has been carried further than on the primary and secondary levels. Two-thirds of the public colleges and universities of the South now admit both colored and white students. Although the proportion is not large—is minute in fact in the Deep South—there are about ten thousand Negro students enrolled in institutions of higher education that were entirely segregated a few years ago. And there are white students in twenty-four of the fifty-two formerly all-Negro colleges.[9]

Considering the number of persons involved, there has not yet been a major desegregation of schools. The steps taken so far have been accompanied by extensive litigation, some merely token compliance with court orders, and, in a few instances, violence. In my judgment, however, the more important fact is that an essentially irreversible process has begun. Although conflicts in Little Rock, New Orleans, Oxford, and elsewhere produced the headline stories, quiet beginnings of desegregation in the schools of Houston, Atlanta, Dallas, Richmond, and Memphis are the more important stories. Conflict one year may be followed by quiet change later; e.g., all three of Little Rock's previously all-white high schools and most of her junior high schools now enroll Negro pupils. During the autumn of 1960, while tension surrounded the two desegregated elementary schools in New Orleans, the people of the city elected a moderate to their school board with a plurality of ten thousand votes over the combined votes of his three segregationist opponents. The citizens of Arkansas in 1960 turned down, by a margin of three to one, an amendment which would have allowed school boards to close schools to avoid desegregation. This vote was a vigorous repudiation of an important part of the program of their segregationist-minded governor.

Although school desegregation is primarily a Southern question, there are many quasi-segregated schools in Northern and Western cities. Segregation in these schools is produced by the concentration of nonwhite families in a few residential areas. A survey made by the American Jewish Committee in 1957 found that 20 percent of the public schools in Chicago, 43 percent in Cincinnati, 22 percent in Cleveland, 21 percent in Detroit, 15 percent in Los Angeles, 20 percent in New York, 27 percent in Philadelphia, and 7 percent in San Francisco had nonwhite majorities. Present population trends are increasing these proportions, sometimes with the consequence that schools become resegregated by neighborhood changes. This situation is not identical with one produced by total and officially enforced segregation; there is a substantial minority of white pupils in many of the schools mentioned above. Yet it cannot be denied that in the large cities of the North and West, a significant proportion of the colored children, and of the Mexican and Puerto Rican children as well, attend schools in which intergroup contact is at a minimum. And the proportion attending such schools is likely to go up as white families move from the cities to suburbs where few or no colored families reside.

A Federal court has ruled, in a case involving New Rochelle, New York, that any segregation which reflects action by a public body, past or present, is now subject to review. The specific reference was to a case dealing with gerrymandering of school zones to increase the likelihood of racially homogeneous schools. The President's Commission on Civil Rights noted, in connection with this decision:

School boards that want to operate their schools in a constitutional manner may have to inquire into the cause of any existing segregation. They may have to prove that zoning lines follow residential patterns by coincidence, not design; that the sites and sizes of schools were not fixed to assure segregation; that racial residential patterns were not officially created in the first instance. Thus *New Rochelle* challenges many school boards in the North and the West which have thought they were immune from attack because existing segregation did not result from school assignment explicitly by race.[10]

Several procedures have been developed by school boards and administrative staffs to try to reduce the number of quasi-segregated schools. Skillful districting, a sort of reverse gerrymandering, can sometimes be used to assign minority-group children to several schools. New York City, Cleveland, and other cities transport several thousand pupils out of their districts in an effort to disperse heavy concentrations of Negro and Puerto Rican children in some schools. A few communities have shifted from the neighborhood concept for elementary schools to a plan calling for the assignment of all first- and second-grade children to one school, third and fourth graders to another, fifth and sixth graders to another. Although this "Princeton Plan" increases problems of transportation, it can reduce the tendency toward segregation in schools. It may, in addition, have significant educational advantages.

Such procedures as these, however, can only slightly reduce school segregation that exists because of the fact that many American cities contain large subcommunities of nonwhites. Significant changes in the school pattern are dependent upon future developments in educational policy, urban renewal programs, housing practices, and the economic position of minority groups. For the most part, *de facto* school segregation in the North is a second-level social problem. Most white families accept the principle of school integration. According to the Gallup Poll,[11] 87 percent of the white parents in the North state that they would not object to sending their children to a school "where a few of the children are colored." (The proportion is 38 percent in the South.) This drops to 56 percent if half the children were colored, with 33 percent saying they would object and 11 percent expressing no opinion. Actions, of course, are not the same as verbal opinions, but they are not necessarily more discriminatory. In fact, the relatively peaceful acceptance of desegregation by most Southern parents and of increases in colored proportions by most Northern parents indicates that wherever clear and firm decisions are made, actions are likely to be *less* discriminatory than opinions. Some parents who accept the principle of school integregration have objected to various means by which it is brought about—transporting children out of their neighborhoods by bus, for example.

Negro parents, on the other hand, are becoming less and less willing to accept *de facto* segregation. School boycotts in New York, Chicago, and Cleveland have served as dramatic protests against the concentration of Negro children into the schools of limited areas, schools which at the same time are often of inferior quality. It seems highly likely that one of the major issues of the last half of the 1960s, so far as minority-majority relations are concerned, will be the growing demand for elimination of *de facto* segregation and the responses to that demand. The increase in the total number of children during this period will complicate the problem, but will also offer opportunities for relocating school boundaries and redesigning school policies.

Churches

It has often been said that "eleven o'clock Sunday morning is the most segregated hour of the week." Although this has been substantially true, changes since World War II have made modification of the statement necessary. There are so many churches in the United States, with such widely divergent practices, that any brief summary is liable to error. However it is to be hoped that citing the following items will be sufficient to convey an accurate impression:

In the South, local congregations, almost without exception, are segregated. Resistance to integration has strong support from some churches and ministers, particularly of the sectarian, fundamentalist variety. Most of the clergy in the middle- and upper-class churches either avoid any reference to the question of segregation or call for Christian understanding without specifying what steps are required at the given moment. Faced with the problem of holding a divided or segregationist-minded congregation together, they turn to less controversial issues.[12]

On the other hand, 80 percent of the Protestant ministers from the South who responded to an inquiry from *Pulpit Digest* supported the Supreme Court decision outlawing school segregation. Ministerial associations in Richmond, Nashville, Atlanta, and other cities have appealed for peaceful desegregation of schools, if not of their own churches. Every major denomination in the South—still excluding the fundamentalist sects—has gone on record as favoring the Supreme Court decision. And individual ministers have been prominent among the few white Southerners who have taken active, and often courageous, parts in the integration process. In 1963, twenty-eight young Methodist ministers joined in a manifesto that proclaimed their belief in "freedom of the pulpit" and opposed "racial discrimination in the state of their birth"—Mississippi. As a result, all were boycotted by their congregations or were otherwise harassed.[13]

In the North, most local congregations are still segregated. As in the South, the churches of the lower classes, of the recent migrants from rural areas—the small "storefront" and other fundamentalists groups—oppose integration. A large majority of the local congregations belonging to the established denominations are also segregated. It should be noted, however, that this is not always a sign of unwillingness to accept colored members. There may be no Negroes or other nonwhites living in the area or they may feel no desire to become associated with a white church. Moreover, a significant minority of the established Northern churches, Protestant and Catholic, now have some interracial character—perhaps about 10 percent. This is a very recent development; most of the desegregation has occurred within the last decade. Usually it means, not that there has been extensive integration, but that a small number of families of Oriental or Negro descent have joined a formerly all-white church. They are usually professional and business people whose education and income are similar to those of the other members. In a few instances, usually in areas of a city where there has been a large increase in the nonwhite population, more extensive integration of congregations, and occasionally of ministerial staffs, has occurred.

Altogether, one can find in these various trends among churches a sensitive index to the currents of desegregation.[14]

Public Accommodations

Generalization in this area is even more difficult and hazardous than in the others we have discussed. There are tens of thousands of publicly and privately owned facilities serving the general public, and their policies range from full integration to total segregation. Despite this diversity, however, I think it is correct to state that there has been extensive desegregation in the use of public accomodations since World War II. What is some of the evidence for this statement?

Before the war, segregation in hotels and restaurants was the rule, even in major Northern cities. Conventions with multiracial membership were able to secure accommodations, but individual colored persons were often denied service. Almost all of the Northern states already had civil rights statutes requiring that all businesses catering to the general public must grant service to everyone, without regard to race, religion, or national origin. Twenty-nine states now have such laws. But the laws were repeatedly violated without penalty. After the war this situation began to change for a number of reasons: The growing economic power of colored Americans made it more costly to neglect them as customers; their increased political participation made it more costly to neglect the enforcement of civil rights statutes; new state and local antidiscrimination commissions have been assigned some responsibility in civil rights matters; and public attitudes are significantly more favorable to integrated facilities. Virtually all of the larger hotels, restaurants, and theaters are now desegregated in the major Northern and Western cities. This is less true of some of the smaller businesses and in the smaller cities.

There has also been desegregation in border cities, particularly in Washington, D.C. Despite the difficulties caused by segregation in the nation's capital, most of its public facilities were segregated until 1950. Without specifying all the details of the shift, let me simply state that, as a result of such forces as administrative action, court decisions, international incidents, and a general change in the climate of opinion, the major hotels and restaurants, the theaters, swimming pools, and—in a somewhat different connection—the schools have been desegregated. To those acquainted with Washington in the early 1950s and before, the speed and extent of the change is truly dramatic. There have been similar if not always such extensive changes in St. Louis, Cincinnati, Louisville, Baltimore, and other border cities.

The least extensive but perhaps the most significant changes have occurred in the South. In a region where there are no state civil rights statutes and where opposition to desegregation is strongest, there have nevertheless been steps taken toward integration of public facilities—steps that were difficult to imagine even five years ago. In 1946, the Supreme Court ruled against segregation in interstate travel and in the terminals connected with it. The purchase of interstate tickets on a nonsegregated basis became standard practice on buses, trains, and airplanes within a few years; changes in the terminals have been slower. Between 1955 and 1957, several decisions by the Supreme Court and other Federal courts invalidated state and local laws requiring segregated seating on public conveyances, and required the integration of public recreational facilities.

These decisions were widely ignored, as we were shown by the spotlight focused on the Freedom Riders. But their protests—and the violence against them—seemed to persuade the Interstate Commerce Commission. In September, 1961, that body issued an order banning segregation in all interstate travel facilities—an order that has been carried out almost without exception.

Perhaps more significant than these developments, which were aided by court and other public decisions, has been the desegregation of commercial places in the middle and upper South and to some degree in the Deep South. The sit-in movement has generated some opposition and violence, but far more often has opened lunch counters, restaurants, hotels, parks, libraries, zoos, and other public facilities to persons of all races, by peaceful demonstration and negotiation. Negro college students, white businessmen, and several private human relations organizations have been largely responsible for this change which, since 1960, has desegregated hundreds of places of public accommodation in almost every Southern state.

Desegregation has not proceeded far in the South, and it is virtually nonexistent in Southern rural areas, but a significant start has been made in the cities.

Arts and Entertainment Media

Because Negroes have played a prominent part in the world of music and entertainment, one is likely to assume that integration has been common in these areas of American life. Actually, integrated groups of musicians or entertainers have been few. Some jazz groups have been interracial; in recent years the Metropolitan Opera Association has hired its first Negro artists; a few symphony orchestras and choral groups have been desegregated; and Negro performers have played some standard, nonstereotyped roles on the stage, in television plays, and in motion pictures. In 1963, one of the results of the vigorous protest movement was the fairly extensive increase in the use of Negroes on television, both in advertisements and on programs.

These are important beginnings. Perhaps of equal interest has been the reduction of the tendency to treat minority-group persons in stereotyped and caricatured ways. It is not always easy to draw a line between an artistic portrayal of the members of a disprivileged group, with their real life problems and struggles, and a caricatured portrayal that grossly distorts and usually defames.

Let me desert the essentially descriptive point of view of this chapter for a moment to offer a moral judgment. To show that there is violence and ugliness in the life of minority persons, as well as tenderness and courage, is mandatory on the artist; but to reproduce a comic or distorted image that exists only in the stereotypes of an unthinking majority is poor art. Sometimes the caricaturing process is defended as part of Americana, to be taken with a touch of humor by those who are the objects of its ridicule. Two things can be said regarding this point of view: Some parts of Americana—the minstrel show, for example—are mediocre as art and as history. Why not let them die out? And the test of humor can gracefully be applied only to oneself. Perhaps the old-fashioned criteria of the gentleman can guide us here. To me, the most important mark of the gentleman is his sensitivity to things that may offend the dignity of another human being. Gracefulness and gentlemanliness apply two ways, of course. It is unfortunate when those who are offended by caricatures resort to recrimination rather than gentle rebuke, to censorship rather than an appeal to high standards of art and human sensitivity. But the greater obligation rests with those who are most secure and most powerful.

Sports

Few types of human endeavor have more objective criteria of excellence than sports. If exclusion on the presumed grounds of lack of preparation or talent is disguised prejudice, it is easily exposed by the facts. In many parts of the country, high school and college athletic teams have been integrated for decades, a fact well underscored by a look at the record books or at an American Olympic team. Since professional football when it appeared, drew most of its players from college teams, it rather quickly hired players regardless of race, although resistance to this policy continued until as late as 1961 on some teams. Such individual sports as boxing have long been used by boys from low-status groups to improve their income and status.

Perhaps the most dramatic step toward integration of sports was Branch Rickey's decision, in 1946, to add a Negro player to the Brooklyn Dodgers. In Jackie Robinson he found an almost ideal person to take the lead. His athletic talent was unquestionable; he was able to take verbal and physical abuse without retaliation and without letting it disturb his playing; yet he also conveyed the impression to those who abused him that he was not accepting their definition of his role, nor was he shrinking from them. When we now see the list of Negro, Puerto Rican, and Mexican stars in the major leagues of American baseball, it is difficult to remember how thoroughly segregation prevailed on the teams only a few years ago. The consequences reach far beyond the sports arena. There are dozens of stars with whom minority-group boys can identify; there is a quickening of pride; there is an increase in equalitarian contact.

In the last few years, the first steps toward desegregation of golf and tennis have been taken, aided by the success of such persons as Althea Gibson on the courts of Wimbledon and Forest Hills. Public golf courses and tennis courts are open to all in most Northern communities and in several cities of the South. Private clubs, however, continue to be segregated in most cases throughout the country.

Conclusion

This brief catalog of the changes that have taken place in American race relations during the last generation can only give a hint of the desegregation process. It is primarily a record of public acts and institutional changes, with little reference to the spirit with which individuals have received and participated in those changes. Individual responses are important of course. When changes are accepted reluctantly, under fear of penalty, the course of events is different from the consequence of a new pattern that is accepted enthusiastically. Yet this contrast can easily be exaggerated, particularly if one is interested in long-run developments. Contemporary sociology emphasizes the extent to which the public definition of events, which is the institutional structure within which group interaction takes place, affects the individual's response. Within the last twenty-five years, as I have tried to show, this public definition, as it applies to race relations, has been drastically changed in the United States. The extent of the change so far has accomplished the reshaping of individual attitudes in such a way that further change becomes more likely.

The fact that the present balance of forces is producing desegregation does not mean that desegregation is inevitable. We can say with some confidence that if present trends continue further desegregation seems likely. But present trends may not continue. Economic prosperity and growth have certainly supported the growth of integration. The rapid development of urban areas and the related heavy migration of minority-group persons, although their effects have been somewhat antithetical, have in general lent support to desegregation. Without trying to list all the variables that affect the speed and direction of change, I would mention at least the following additional ones: the international situation, the presence of organized groups, the appearance of leaders with strategic skills, and the strength of the movement that is trying to extend and improve education. Most of these influences support desegregation now and they seem likely to in the future.

There are, however, some forces that may work in the opposite direction *if* they continue to operate: Although the concentration of Negroes in the rural counties of the South is greatly reduced, there is a strong tendency for them to be reconcentrated in the center of the large industrial cities. During the first 150 years of the nation's history, there was a steady decline in the proportion of the population that was nonwhite. Since 1940, this trend has been reversed and we can expect a small increase in the proportion of the population that is nonwhite—perhaps from 11.3 percent in 1960 to 14 percent in 2000. This does not seem to me to be a very important variable among those affecting desegregation, but if other factors were blocking further integration, the demographic situation might support them. And finally, the strength of isolationist and other hostile movements among minorites—the Black Muslims are the most important current example—must be taken into account. Virtually all minority-group organizations now support desegregation, but this would not necessarily continue to be the case if the process of integration were to stop or to slow down significantly.

What then can one say in summary regarding the prospects for continuing desegregation? It seems highly probable that further extensive desegregation will take place. The three-hundred-year era during which race symbols have been important in determining a person's life chances and in group relations in most of the Western world is coming to an end. Its fundamental roots in slavery, in conquest, in colonialism and imperialism, in the sharp cultural differences often found, in plantation economies, and in the Civil War are all broken. (It is by no means impossible, however, that a reciprocal racism, already apparent in some measure, will develop, as more *nonwhite* peoples rise to military, economic, and political power. This would be one of history's bitter ironies were it to occur even as the European and European-derived peoples were eliminating race from their perspectives. Lessons learned too late are not uncommon in human experience.)

Within the United States race lines are fading. That does not mean that a Negro will be elected mayor of New York, or of Birmingham, tomorrow, although the former may not be many years away. Racial disprivilege will outlive the twentieth century, but in less and less extensive ways. If the United States takes as many steps toward full integration in the next twenty-five years as she has in the preceding twenty-five—and this seems fully likely—the country will have accomplished a major social transformation, deeply affecting the whole course of its development, within a half century. Seldom are such vital reorganizations accomplished so swiftly.

If this statement is near the mark, we are led to two further questions which take us beyond the primarily descriptive and analytic perspective we have maintained until now: Where do we want to go? And how best can we get there? These are questions of morality and of strategy, without which the study of a social problem is incomplete. In particular, an issue as significant as the place of minority groups in a complex society can be meaningfully explored only by adding moral and strategic considerations to those of analysis. To those aspects of the question, therefore, we now will turn.

6

GOALS IN INTERGROUP RELATIONS

Toward what goals should a society seek to move in the relationships between minority and majority groups? This is a more complicated moral question than it may seem at first glance. Each of us may believe in mutually contradictory values, but we may not be aware of their contradiction until we undertake new action with regard to them. Then we discover that to support one value is to deny another. There are disagreements between individuals and groups over means more often than over ends. But this is an excessively sharp distinction, for the end we seek today becomes a means for tomorrow's goal, and the means we adopt strongly influence what the end will be. Moreover, the presumed agreement on ends, despite disagreements over methods, may well disguise, even from ourselves, an actual clash of values. "When people agree on an end and disagree on the means, someone must be ignorant of the means to the end or mistaken about the extent of the agreement on ends."[1] As we learn more about the consequences of various processes in majority-minority relations, disagreements over method will decrease, but the effect may in part be to expose more fundamental disagreements over ends than we knew existed.

This problem could be approached descriptively. That is, I could say: This is what various other people say they want and these are the methods they support. . . . We could then introduce various sociological and psychological correlates by indicating who supports which goals and methods and noting the variation by class, level of education, region of the country, religion, and other variables.

In place of this I will adopt a more personal approach in this chapter, in the hope that a clear statement of one person's outlook may be a useful point of departure for the kind of moral commentary that must precede and accompany any effort to resolve a social problem.

Leys has observed that such consensus as we have in intergroup relations in the United States is more negative than positive. There is a large measure of agreement in opposing "warmongering totalitarians" and severe discrimination. But there is less agreement on what we support. Are all lines of distinction among groups sources of weaknesses in a democratic society? Or are some distinctions acceptable and even desirable? If the latter, by what criteria do we determine which forms of segregation and group differentiation are permissible? How much and what kinds of pluralism do we want? To ask the question in a slightly different way: What is public and what is private? Almost everybody supports the idea of the separation of church and state and believes that free choice of one's religious associates and beliefs is desirable. Are segregated parochial schools therefore desirable? Is this any different from a segregated neighborhood based on the private right to choose one's neighbors? We shall explore this question in its relationship to the concept of pluralism below.

There are many value questions associated with method also. Leys points out that there is strong opposition to power-enforced change in industry and elsewhere, an emphasis on the value of discussion, a tendency to idealize persuasion. "It is asserted that uncooperative folk would voluntarily cooperate if given a little more time and a little better opportunity to understand the situation."[2] Suppose, however, that this means the perpetuation for an indefinite period of something one believes unjust? Should the coercions available to government be used? We employ them in many areas without hesitation—to collect taxes or punish criminals, for example. Are they equally appropriate in the effort to reduce discrimination? (Note that this is a double question: Should the force of law and government be used? And if used, under what conditions, and to what degree is it effective?) Some persons value peace over justice; or they may say that justice is impossible without peace—therefore we must not try to reduce discrimination by force. Others value justice over peace; or they may believe that no peace is secure without justice—and therefore it is good to use such coercions as are necessary to reduce discrimination. Either position, if asserted in a doctrinaire way, seems to me to be in error. I would incline, however, toward the latter. For the choice is not actually between coercion and its absence; it is between the private coercions of individuals and groups which harm their fellows and the public coercions which seek to establish equality of treatment.

A third value problem is quite complex in its ramifications. Let us suppose that every individual had complete equality of opportunity with every other; no member of a minority group suffered undue handicap; the capable, the energetic, the lucky—from whatever group—got ahead. This would mean that the slow-witted, the handicapped, those lacking in social grace would be ". . . doomed to a sad existence, regardless of race, nationality, or creed."[3] Is that the good society? Or is charity as well as equality of opportunity a virtue? Are those who were fortunate enough to inherit high capabilities somehow to be preferred over those whose talents are lesser? America's individualism inclines her to answer yes to this last question, but we ought to note that many societies have been able to achieve a good life for *some* of their members. Having arrived at the possibilities of economic affluence, perhaps we need a higher goal: more concern for the goodness of life even for the untalented. I mention this only to suggest that if we solve the moral problems connected with discrimination against minority-group members, we shall not be lacking in still further challenging and important problems to struggle with.

The Paradox of Integration and Pluralism

Perhaps we can approach the problem of goals in a helpful way by examining the idea of pluralism in its relationship to integration on one hand and minority-group discrimination on the other. Can a democratic society allow and encourage distinctive groups without running serious risks that some will become the targets of hostility and discrimination? How heterogeneous can we be without inviting group conflict?

In an article in the *Encyclopedia of Social Science,* Edward Sapir describes in a delightful way the mutually contradictory functions of fashion. In the changing, mobile societies where fashion prevails, many persons are torn between a desire to be different, to stand out in the crowd, and a desire to belong, to feel the security of group acceptance. Fashion, which is custom in the guise of departure from custom, is an effort to negotiate betweeen these two desires. A woman is dismayed at the thought of appearing in public in a hat that is not stylish at the given time and place—with a brim too wide or not wide enough, with feathers and dangles when simplicity is the mode. Thus she seeks to belong, to be like the others. The only thing that would dismay her more than excessive difference would be to discover that she is wearing a hat exactly like another's. To put the problem in terms of the theme of this chapter, she wants integration, but she also wants pluralism. Or, in Sapir's words, she seeks the invigorating but comforting feeling of "adventurous safety."

Lionel Trilling has somewhere expressed the same idea by noting the tension between the desire for nonconformity and the desire to belong securely to a group. We resolve the issue by deciding to be nonconformists together.

Thus the topic of this chapter has wide applicability; but our concern is only with its relevance to the study of minority groups. We have defined integration as a situation in which the members of a society, regardless of their race, religion, or national origin, move freely among one another, sharing the same opportunities and the same privileges and facilities on an equal basis. Thus defined, the term carries to some degree a connotation of assimilation: the loss of separating group identities, with differentiation only on an individual basis.

Pluralism, of course, means something quite different. Membership in distinctive ethnic, religious, or cultural groups is accepted and even applauded. Pluralistic societies pride themselves on the freedom granted to diverse groups to preserve different cultural heritages, support various religions, speak different languages, and develop independent associations. This freedom is qualified only by the requirement of loyalty to the prevailing political and economic systems.

It is scarcely necessary to document the assertion that strong networks of private associations, based on the ideal of pluralism, do not weaken the cohesion of a democratic society but actually strengthen it. Such networks serve both to relate an individual, through groups that are close and meaningful to him, to the large, complex society, and also to protect him from excessive encroachments on his freedom by that society. A totalitarian state begins at once to try to destroy private associations—free trade unions, independent churches, autonomous news agencies, or lingual and cultural groups different from the majority—because they are bulwarks against domination by the state.

If these propositions are correct, they raise serious questions in connection with current trends in the United States: Does a democratic society require integration among its diverse peoples; or are minority groups actually an expression of legitimate pluralism? Does the process of desegregation threaten the balance of integration and pluralism? Has "segregation" been made into a loaded word that supports an attack on a desirable pluralism? Or, to reverse the tone of these questions: Can we have ethnic, religious, and racial pluralism without creating or preserving minority groups? Can we be religiously tolerant, and yet active in our own churches; patriotic, but not ethnocentric and chauvinistic; closely identified with our own group, without feeling hostility to others? Some of the evidence seems to show that much of mankind is still tribalistic in its outlook, and that the abolition of old group identities is necessary to promote harmony between people. But there are also evidences of intergroup cooperation. If we can have pluralism without conflict, around what symbols of identification should pluralistic centers be formed? Can we agree on the criteria by means of which it is possible to distinguish between undemocratic discrimination and valuable cultural differentiation?

I have no hope of answering these questions definitively, but if I can raise them in a useful way, you may be led to a productive reexamination of the issues involved. Perhaps the basic task is to explore the place of minority groups in complex societies and to distinguish them from pluralistic groups.

Although we shall consider only the United States, the issues involved are international. In fact, excepting only war and the threat of war, perhaps no other topic arouses more interest around the world than the treatment of minority groups. As we noted in Chapter 3, there are few societies in the world today without minority groups—groups that are singled out by the rulers, or individuals, or both—for discriminatory treatment. Needless to say, the United States is prominent on the list of such societies, both because of her serious minority problems and because of her position as leader of the free world.

I believe it is no exaggeration to say that how America is to deal with the question of minorities is the most significant internal problem before us at this point in history. It would be overly dramatic to suggest that an issue has its moment on stage, as a democratic society struggles to become a fully unified nation; but a case can be made for reading history that way. We have moved from the struggle for independence, to conflict over universal suffrage and representation, to the battle for unity, to the problem of the place of the worker in an industrial society, to the issue of setting a subsistence floor under the whole economy, to the task of uniting with a world suddenly made small. None of these issues—particularly, of course, the last—has been resolved; but the institutional framework for their resolution has been invented. And in this context we are coming to see that the full solution of each of the previous great issues depends to an important degree on the wise incorporation of minority groups into national life. This problem, of course, is not new, for we have been a nation of minorities from the beginning. But if our minorities are "Old American," as most of them are, serious attention to their place in society is not old. It would not be much of an exaggeration to say that twenty-five years ago the nation was largely unmindful of what this democratic society had to offer to persons of Negro, Mexican, Indian, or Oriental descent. Yet, today the issue presses in on us. Our complacency is broken. A truly massive migration; a revolution of rising expectations, applying not simply to the Congo, to China, or to Egypt, but to our own minorities; war and cold war emphasis on our democratic leadership; and many other forces have made the minorities question unavoidable. We have slowly developed new ideas and inventions in human relations, but the process is painful. It is not easy to get rid of an old institution.

Integration and Pluralism in Hawaii

One way to approach the problem of the relationship between pluralism, integration, and discrimination in America is to examine what is perhaps our most pluralistic state, Hawaii. By observing the relationships among the numerous racial, religious, and ethnic groups in Hawaii, we can have in mind a kind of measuring stick against which other parts of the nation can be compared. We can also learn from a study of this state something about the extent to which group difference must mean discrimination and the extent to which reduction of discrimination implies the loss of group distinctiveness.

From the mainland, of course, Hawaii performs some subtle functions in our harried lives. It carries some of the load of our erotic imagery—the Polynesian maiden by the limpid pool—and offers some relief from our mingled fears and guilt over tense intergroup relations in the rest of the nation. On the Islands these functions are somewhat less obvious. To some degree the imagery has to be pushed back to Tahiti (and in Tahiti, perhaps to Bora Bora).

The intergroup relations picture in Hawaii is somewhat more complicated than it appears at first glance. Little time need be spent describing the population of the state. Roughly speaking, it is one-third Caucasian (a group that now includes the Portuguese and most of the Puerto Ricans), one-third Japanese, one-sixth Hawaiian (a mixture, for only a small proportion of this one-sixth is full-blooded Polynesian), 11 percent Filipino, 6 percent Chinese, and a small proportion of Koreans, Samoans, and Negroes. It is the only state in the union with a non-Caucasian majority.

To say that these groups live in perfect harmony would be an exaggeration. There are some ethnic prejudices and discriminatory practices, expressed largely in a kind of ethnic hierarchy. I shall not undertake here to offer an explanation for the ranking, except to say that it is based to an important degree on the chronology of migrations to the Islands. Each succeeding wave of migrants, with the exception of mainland Caucasians, has entered the status structure at the bottom. The groups that came to Hawaii earlier, therefore, have moved up to higher-status levels in a way similar to the rise of European immigrants in the rest of the United States. Chronology alone, of course, does not account for the present rough correlation between ethnic group and class position. The occupational and class origins of the migrants are involved, and variation in cultural preparation for life in a literate and technologically developed society must be considered. Racial prejudice, as such, plays only an unimportant part in producing the status patterns.

The result of these and other influences has been to place most Filipinos and Negroes near the bottom at the present time, along with some Puerto Ricans. Equally disadvantaged are most of the full-blooded Hawaiians who struggle with a problem not unlike that of many American Indians. They are unable to live in their aboriginal ways and yet are blocked from participation in the larger society by their own values and by the biases they meet. They feel some resentment, particularly toward the Japanese, who have moved rapidly ahead of them.

Above these groups are the part-Hawaiians and the Japanese, many of whom are moving with great speed up the educational, occupational, and income ladders. The Chinese, earlier migrants to the Islands, are probably further ahead still. Their high status is slightly qualified by a touch of "anti-Semitism," however, for in Hawaii, as in lands of the Western Pacific, the business successes of the Chinese have sometimes led to their identification as "the Jews of the Orient." That the Chinese are often believed to be crafty, intelligent, ambitious, and materialistic tells us more about intergroup relations than about their personal characteristics. (It is interesting to note that somewhat similar stereotypes of high-status minorities have existed in different times and places. Scotsmen, Yankees, Greeks, and other groups have been or are regarded in terms similar to those used for Chinese and Jews in some settings.)

The Caucasians, who are somewhat resentfully referred to as Haoles, are no longer the clearly dominant group. Most of the large business operations are still in their hands, but the overwhelming power of the Big Five—the shipping, pineapple, and sugar companies that formerly dominated the economy—has been somewhat dispersed since the war. The average income of the Chinese is now a little higher than that of the Haoles. Statehood has increased the importance of the political process and strengthened the position of the non-Caucasians.

The older generations of some of these groups, particularly the Chinese, Japanese, and Haoles, have taught their children some sense of separation and even of prejudice against other groups. This is partly the result of a desire to preserve distinctive cultural heritages and partly an expression of disdain for those who have not yet shown much talent for status improvement in an urban world. At the University of Hawaii, where I secured responses to a lengthy questionnaire from five hundred persons, most students feel vaguely guilty about their tendencies toward categorical judgments. They have become self-conscious about their stereotypes, and most of them freely cross racial and ethnic lines in their friendship choices. Yet the results of the ethnocentric aspects of their training are still apparent—with reference, for example, to Filipinos. There are few Filipino students at the University. (Although they are now moving up the status ladder, Filipinos are relative newcomers to the islands; most still occupy low-status jobs in the plantation areas.) Since many of the University students are from Honolulu, they have little direct contact with Filipinos. This does not prevent a large proportion, however, from "knowing" that Filipinos are quick-tempered, revengeful, impulsive, musical, and quarrelsome. These were the adjectives most likely to be overselected (chosen at a rate higher than would be true on a random basis) as characteristic of Filipinos. These adjectives were selected from a long list more than four times as frequently as one would have expected as a result of random choice. Yet it should also be said that over half of the students would welcome a Filipino as a close friend and less than 10 percent expressed strong hostility.

Although these observations qualify the view that Hawaii is a state almost lacking intergroup hostility, the total picture remains one of relatively little stereotyping and discrimination. The light animosities that do exist are based more nearly on class differences than on race or ethnic origin. They are projected downward, for the most part, to the lower prestige groups. The Caucasians, however, are not universally applauded. An undertone of resentment is well expressed by the story of Japanese workers, furiously shoveling the hot lava that was pouring down the mountain from a volcano, trying to prevent it from rolling into a village. A Haole observer, who stood nearby to watch the spectacle, remarked to a friend: "That lava looks hot as hell!" "Oh, those Haoles," said one Japanese worker to another, "they've been everywhere."

For many Caucasians in Hawaii, racial and ethnic lines are utterly unimportant. But there are patches of exclusiveness and old-fashioned prejudice. Although many professional positions are held by persons of Oriental descent, there are some high-level business positions not fully open to non-Caucasians. There also remain a few segregated streets and golf, canoe, and business clubs. To some degree these represent the continuation of the old order when the territory was a plantation with white overlords and Oriental and Polynesian field hands—to put it, of course, all too simply. That order is gone, but not all the ideas have changed. Some younger Caucasians also defend these segregated patches with a somewhat plaintive feeling, as they see how things are going—"We can't let the upstarts take over everything."

One would draw a false picture if he did not mention these things.

Yet they truly seem incidental. The impressive fact is that the state, only a short way removed from near feudalism, is very nearly integrated—residentially, economically, educationally. This does not mean there are no class differences, for the class range is as wide in Hawaii as elsewhere. Nor does it imply that ethnic lines do not to some degree correlate with class. It means that categorical barriers against a person simply on grounds of group membership are rare. Even intermarriage is common. Between 1957 and 1959, one-third of all marriages in Hawaii were between persons of different ethnic or racial groups. Thirty-five percent of the babies during that period were born to couples of mixed racial or ethnic origin.[4]

Segregation and Pluralism

The evidence of integration does not lead to the conclusion that group identity is lost in Hawaii. Perhaps the keenest impression that one gets in the state is the remarkable blend of integration and pluralism. Many Buddhist temples have established Sunday schools, and the children sing, "Buddha loves me, this I know." But some Buddhist priests return to Japan to study the classic ways of their particular sect, in order to preserve them without contamination in the new land. Although the several ethnic and class groups are not equally represented, the University is a blend of all the peoples in the state. Yet there are Chinese and Caucasian and Japanese sororities such as would be banned on some mainland campuses. When beauty contest time arrives, pluralism is delightfully upheld by the participation of candidates from each group, plus a cosmopolitan, to uphold the value of the integration. And then not one but seven winners are chosen.

This, then, is the outstanding fact. Despite patchy discrimination, Hawaii has an amazing amount of unity in diversity. Somehow the state has preserved distinctive groups with visibly different subcultures, yet maintains integration among them. It is perhaps too early to know whether this is a purely temporary state of affairs— the fortunate balance of forces at a moment in time—or a surface phenomenon that hides deep rifts or, oppositely, hides powerful forces toward uniformity. However this may be, the present

Hawaiian situation can be of great significance to the whole country, not because it will cause us on the mainland to change, but because it shows us a pattern of what *can* take place. Even though its causal importance is small, Hawaii can be an effective symbol at a time when America is experiencing in acute form the age-old problem of integration versus pluralism. How does a democratic society maintain a sense of unity at the same time that it permits, or perhaps even encourages, diversity? Does the idea of pluralism support some forms of segregation? If not, can distinctive cultures and points of view be maintained to enrich the nation and broaden the public debate? But if so, can certain forms of segregation be prevented from supporting undemocratic discrimination?[5]

This is truly a difficult and paradoxical question. It is not always easy to distinguish between arbitrary and discriminatory segregation and legitimate pluralism. We want to support pride in one's group, the protection of its contribution to the national life, a meaningful tie to one's parents. Yet these can be related to a separatism that splits a society in serious ways. When is a line of distinction an undesirable segregation as contrasted with a legitimate pluralism? Let me undertake to state in a formal way a few basic principles that may help us to answer this question.

First, it is an undesirable segregation, as contrasted with a legitimate pluralism, when a line of distinction is related in hidden ways to other lines of separation. A men's club, justified on the grounds that one has a right to pick his friends, often has covert or even obvious significance in politics and the higher job market. To be excluded from the club is to be kept, not only from a friendship circle, but from important economic and political participation. Housing segregation, often justified on much the same grounds, is frequently—one can almost say universally—related to segregation in schools, parks, and jobs. Above all, housing segregation separates the child from access to the larger culture whose complexities he must master if he is to improve his situation. We should note in addition that many "social" clubs and neighborhoods are large groups of people, many of whom are strangers to each other. Members are picked, not because of congeniality, but because they belong to the right category. Even in a small town, one can live for years on a block and have only the most casual contact with many fellow residents. Seldom does one have any part in choosing his neighbors.

Let me ask the question again: When does a line of distinction become undesirable segregation; when is it legitimate pluralism? When the separation is systematic or total it is undesirable segregation. It is one thing, for example, for a city to have a few lily-white neighborhoods. It is another thing to have massive ghettoization. That a non-Caucasian finds it difficult or impossible to buy a house in some areas of Makiki Heights in Honolulu may represent an unfortunate snobbishness, but its significance is vastly different from total exclusiveness in a city. Patches of segregation may be acceptable in a democracy, in the name of individual freedom—freedom even to be snobbish, however much one may impoverish his life thereby. However, systematic segregation which allows minority-group members few escape hatches produces vastly more difficult problems for the minorities and for the total community.

A third answer to the same question: When segregation is designed to keep certain groups out, rather than to get or keep persons with certain characteristics in—that is, when it is exclusive rather than inclusive—it is an undesirable separation. Those who defend a white neighborhood do not say: We want to get all whites, or all those whites who are of a given educational and economical level, in. They say: We want to keep nonwhites out.

Finally, segregation is unacceptable when it is not based on some generally recognized cultural or functional distinction. When engineers are kept out of the AMA, or non-Catholics from the Newman Club, no one objects. Exclusion of well-qualified Negroes from the Metropolitan or Cosmos Clubs in Washington, however, can scarcely be explained in cultural or functional terms.

These principles are neither exhaustive nor mutually exclusive, but together they may be helpful in making the moral decision so critically necessary today. Perhaps they can be summarized in these words: Separation is legitimate in a democracy when it is freely chosen and not coerced, when it does not deny any group access to the mainstream of the culture while giving others an advantage, when it does not so warp the personalities of some—by denying them hope and the opportunity to learn the skills and values of the society—that not only they but the whole nation suffers.

The Results of Segregation

There is probably substantial, but not complete, agreement among Americans on these principles. There is less agreement on how they can and should be applied to our current situation. It is relatively easy to apply them to Hawaii, where, for a number of reasons associated with the history of the Islands, their relevance is easy to see. It is vastly more difficult to apply these principles to minority-majority relations on the mainland, where we struggle painfully with problems associated with arbitrary segregation and discrimination based largely on race.

Some American minorities are primarily pluralistic, as we have used that term. For many Indians and Jews, for example, the preservation of a distinctive tradition within the framework of a larger national unity is the desired goal. We have only touched upon that issue here; but we must remember that pluralistic integration requires different policies from those that promote assimilation. We are primarily interested here, however, in the process of redefinition of the place of Negroes in American society. There are some, of course, who resist the current process of change because they "know" that the white man is superior or because they want to preserve some advantage. But there are others who are troubled by the problem of pluralism. They ask, without understanding perhaps, but also without malice: Why can't Negroes (or, less urgently, other nonwhite or ethnically different groups) be content with their own schools, residential areas, churches, and work situations? And in the background we hear a small but growing number of Negroes—many of them members of the Black Muslims—answer: Indeed, why not? Their response is aggressive and divisive, however, not pluralistic. The answer we seek is complicated, but two aspects stand out:

First, the country cannot afford to allow them to "be content with their own . . ." because this implies a continuing separation from the mainstream of American culture. And it is just this separation that has produced such grave problems among Negroes as we face today. The separation began when their ancestors were torn from their homelands, deprived of any chance to maintain their cultures, and had their family patterns disrupted. The disasters of slavery were perpetuated by the semifeudal system that followed—a system that has only recently been weakened. One of America's important tasks is to bring more Negroes, and the members of other disprivileged groups, into full participation in the total culture. Until we do, we shall continue to suffer such painful consequences of their isolation as a heavy crime rate, the loss of skills, the relative lack of educational disciplines and values, and carelessness with public and private property.

These consequences were kept down, or at least affected the total society less severely, so long as most Negroes were isolated and helpless on the plantation. This has led some persons to argue, with nostalgia, that those were better times. Perhaps they were, if one fears conflict more than he approves justice. We have noted, however, that to many it seems better to struggle for justice even at the cost of some conflict. This issue is academic in any event, for Negroes have left the farm; they are dreaming the American dream; they are no longer docile. We could not have developed a mobile, industrial, urban society without this happening. Our clear choice now is to bear the costs of frustrating the drive toward equality of colored Americans (and we are beginning to see how heavy those costs can be) or to do everything possible to speed their absorption, with full hope and opportunity, into all aspects of national life.

Closely related to the first is the second aspect of my answer to the question: Why cannot they be content with their own . . . ? Negroes do not have a distinctive tradition and culture. They are not a group in any meaningful definition of the term. The slavery experience smashed their native heritage but gave them only particles of a new one. As old Americans, they must either share the full culture with others, or they must invent a new one. And this we certainly know: An impoverished, frustrated, angry collectivity invents a poor culture. Built on isolation and resentment, it is more likely to be an attack on the established way of life than a creative new one—a contraculture[6] that denies the old values without having anything to put in their place. Our difficult task, therefore, is to make possible and to insist upon, not to prevent, the entry of Negroes and our other disprivileged minorities, into full participation in American life.

Insofar as we fail in this task, we can expect an increase in the strength of such movements as the Black Muslims, a group much in the news in recent months. Although this movement began over thirty years ago, and was preceded by such protests as the one led by Marcus Garvey, its present strength can be understood only by reference to the contemporary scene. Most Negroes are now fully in touch with the American dream of equal opportunity for all; yet many of them are deeply frustrated. They are disillusioned with Christian churches, including their own. The rise of the African states has brought a stir of excitement, not because American Negroes feel a direct connection with the Africans, but because they are dramatic new developments led by colored men. Since an impoverished and semiliterate group has few weapons with which to fight, an exciting religious movement that promises both earthly and heavenly salvation has great appeal.

Let me sketch some aspects of the Black Muslim sect among American Negroes, drawing on the excellent books by Lincoln and Essien-Udom.[7] Since one runs the risk, in examining a particular movement, of exaggerating its importance, let me state explicitly that at the moment the Black Muslims seem much less important than the NAACP, the Urban League, the Congress of Racial Equality, Martin Luther King's Southern-Christian Leadership Conference, other churchs—or Christian forces—the labor movement, and other influences. Yet the Muslims throw onto a large screen, where they are easy to see, some of the hidden results of American race relations—results it is well for us to try to understand.

Professor Lincoln describes the Black Muslims as "an intensely dedicated, tightly disciplined block of more than 100,000 American Negroes, convinced that they have learned the ultimate truth and ready to make any sacrifice it may demand of them."[8] The "ultimate truth" is that the white man's civilization is decadent and his personal morality poor. The black man is destined to rule the earth. He must recognize his Moslem origins, throw the white man off his neck ("Why integrate with a dying man?"), and build a new life. Although violence has rarely broken out, there is a severely aggressive tone in the teachings of the sect. Few movements in the United States have been so explicitly and fully antiwhite as this one.

This is not a Sunday religion. Every Muslim is required to attend at least two services a week and to give generously—sometimes as much as one-third of his annual income. They are encouraged to live respectably with their families, without gambling, drinking, smoking, buying on credit, or overeating—disciplines that raise their standards of living and leave them a margin with which to propagate the faith. Most members are functionally illiterate rural migrants to the cities; most are youthful, male semiskilled workers. Some have been recruited in prisons. The Muslim temples and businesses are built in the heart of the black ghettoes of the large cities—areas largely neglected by the major Christian churches. The sect is a repudiation of Christianity, as a white man's religion; yet its appeal is close to classic Christianity: it propounds a way to a personal rebirth and a new identity. By acquiring, through the Muslim symbolism, a new name, a new homeland, a new religion, disprivileged and self-hating persons acquire hope and confidence.

The movement has its frightening aspects. There is much talk of hatred and violence. Its policy is explicitly and outwardly divisive. In unintended ways, however, it also holds promise. The ideology and practices of the Black Muslims strengthen the family. It encourages thrift, honesty, and discipline on the job. It has reached a number of criminals and delinquents who were unmoved by other appeals. It furnishes symbolic outlets for hostilities that might otherwise be highly destructive. Before we can weigh its consequences, we need to know what alternative forms of response it replaces. Does it draw its support from those who otherwise would engage in thoughtful political activity, disciplined sit-in movements, or the work of the NAACP? Or does it recruit from those whose response to the burdens of being a lower-class Negro in America today might otherwise be personal demoralization or crime? The latter seems more nearly true at this moment.

Seen in this light, the Black Muslims are not nearly so fearful as they sound. But will the unintended and favorable results I have mentioned be the predominant ones in the long run? These indirect gains have to be put alongside the serious losses—the promotion of hatred, the tendency to violence, the restimulation of the extremism of the segregationists, who can see in the Muslim movement justification for their own beliefs and actions. In a pattern common to the history of sects, the group has now been split by the suspension of Malcolm X, one of its most influential leaders. He had plans to organize a Black Nationalist Party. More recently, however, he has renounced his racist views and expressed support for classic Muslim universalism.

Whether the potential gains or the divisive influences will predominate depends far more upon the process of integration in American society than on intrinsic qualities of the movement. The Black Muslims today are only 100,000 persons; but millions more watch and wait. Whether the movement withers away, as others have before it, or is transformed into a constructive force, or grows into a major destructive influence depends upon America's success in reducing the soul-searing frustration that caused it.

We would be wise to think of the Muslims as illustrative of the consequences of discrimination. Our objective should be, not to suppress such movements, but to change the conditions that produce them.

There are other movements far less fully the results of discrimination that require some qualification of my earlier statement that "Negroes do not have a distinctive tradition and culture." By that phrase one can emphasize the fact that Negroes are old American, that they express only rudiments of the African traditions of their ancestors, that they share and participate in the general culture. But this probably underestimates the consequences of the fact that for generations they have shared a common fate, have suffered similar discrimination, and have struggled with the same frustrations. Although colored Americans are not a group, in the sense of an organized body of interacting persons, they have become what we can call a "community of suffering." They have ways of expressing and dealing with their suffering that have developed into cultural forms, passed on to each new generation through socialization in largely segregated groups. America has witnessed, therefore, a culture-building process. We see it in artistic forms, particularly in jazz and folk music, but also in literature, the dance, and drama. It is expressed in religion. It is vividly shown in the nonviolent approach to the campaign for civil rights—an approach that owes a great deal to classic Christianity and to Gandhi, but which has been shaped also out of Negro experience in the United States.

As a result of this culture-building process, a few Negroes have begun to become separatist in a way that is different from that of the Black Muslims, yet expresses some of the same disillusionment with integration and with the values and motives of the dominant group. What is so good, they are asking, about the white man's society, his TV and movie culture, his shady business morality, his religious piety so unmatched by religious action? Laughing at the old cliché, some are saying with James Baldwin: I do not want to marry your sister; I just want to get you off my back. In this development one sees some beginnings of what one might call positive pluralism, as contrasted with the reflexive pluralism and separatism of the Muslims and most earlier Negro movements.

Conclusion

These last trends which I have mentioned, however, are exceptions to the basically integrationist perspective of the civil rights movement. The continued separation of racial minorities in the United States is not, except in small degree, an expression of pluralism. It is a product of their minority status and the discrimination it entails. For a group to play a part in a meaningful pluralism, its members must share a viable tradition and a wish for its preservation and development. It is not enough for them to be bound together by a distinction which has lost its historic significance, and it certainly is not enough to be identified by an arbitrary distinction that has no basis in cultural history or contemporary choice.

Even the kind of pluralism found in Hawaii today should not be looked upon as sacrosanct. One's cultural and national origins still affect his life in significant ways despite a great deal of interaction across ethnic lines. But such distinctive subcultural experiences may not continue for many more generations. It is not easy to maintain a style of life, however dignified and valuable it was at its point of origin, in the vastly different setting of a cosmopolitan city in another society. The decline of distinctive traditions, however, need not be a loss. What would impoverish Hawaii and the whole nation would be the loss of contributions from each of the separate groups to the new and heterogeneous culture of modern society. Perhaps our emphasis should be not on historic pluralism, with its tendency toward rigidity and orientation to the past, but on a *contemporary pluralism.* By that phrase I seek to emphasize the contribution of many historic traditions to a new and diverse culture; but I seek also to stress the value of freedom for individuals and new groups— freedom to choose from the variety and to create new cultural syntheses.[9]

Hawaii has moved a long way from segregation and prejudice toward historic pluralism. Indeed, her complex intermingling of peoples takes her close to contemporary pluralism. The developments there during the last half century clearly show that diversity of race and culture need not be a barrier to integration. When the tests we have proposed are applied to the lines of separation in Hawaii, these lines are shown to be substantially, if not completely, legitimate by democratic standards. For here, separate social groups do not serve, to any strong degree, covert economic and political functions, separation is not massive or total; separate groups tend to be inclusive rather than exclusive; and they are based in most instances on significant cultural differences.

Race relations on the mainland, however, fail the tests we have proposed at almost every point. Here, separation is an expression, not of pluralism, but of discrimination. The task of a democratic society, therefore, is to make possible and to insist upon, not to prevent, the entry of Negroes and other disprivileged minorities into full participation in American life.

From our various perspectives, it is difficult to see the full complexity of this task. Some liberals, playing down the harm done by segregation and discrimination, make the minority-group members the heroes of the struggle while dominant-group members are the villains. There are indeed minority-group heroes—persons of amazing accomplishments in the face of great odds. But there are also heroic white men. Is it not better to see us all in our common humanity—members of a species with none too good a heart or head—struggling with grievous problems? If the social evils of segregation and discrimination are as monstrous as the liberals say—and I believe they are—then they must create some monstrous facts—as unhappily they do.

The conservative emphasizes those very facts. What he fails to see are the social practices and institutions that created and preceded those facts. He takes them simply as given. He sees a school deteriorate, as sometimes happens, when it is flooded with children with no educational tradition who come from impoverished, segregated backgrounds. He knows the comparative rates of crime. There is no need to deny such facts. But we do need to ask where they came from and how they can be removed. When we see a small Negro or Puerto Rican or Mexican child we know that destructive patterns are not preordained in him. Yet we are caught in a vicious cycle so long as we use the contemporary facts as justification for refusal to change the very conditions which produced those facts. I do not want to minimize the difficulties. Every step toward integration is painful, because we must enlarge the circle of interaction and participation of persons many of whom have not—for want of opportunity—absorbed the full range of the community's values. But it is futile to say: Pull yourself up by your own bootstraps and then we will integrate. The social steps have to be taken first—as an act of faith, if you will.

Happily, the act of faith is supported by many facts. Many minority-group persons, caught in deeply disprivileged circumstances, have nevertheless broken out, with the support of an exceptional parent, a friendly businessman, a superior mind, a religious faith— the sources of such an accomplishment are numerous. So deep is the commitment of most minority-group members to American values that every small gain yields surprising dividends. This may not long be the case. In the midst of a worldwide struggle for freedom, their hopes have been aroused as never before. Continued frustration of their aspirations will lead only to an increase in extremist views and resentful actions.

THE REDUCTION OF DISCRIMINATION:

problems of strategy

In the preceding chapter we described a goal that included both integration and pluralism. The moral commentary was offered, not to persuade you, but to encourage you to explore the value questions with care. Recognizing that in such a brief statement I left many issues unresolved, I will nevertheless assume in this chapter that we have a substantial amount of agreement on goals. As a minimum let us agree upon this: No one's life chances should be affected by his race, his religion, or his national or class origin.

Our task now is to investigate problems of strategy: How can we best move toward those goals? Ought major attention be devoted to changing the attitudes of prejudiced persons? What is the place of legal and judicial action? Do sit-ins, freedom rides, protest marches, and picket lines change the situation? In a brief statement we cannot answer such difficult and important questions. My hope will be to raise them in a helpful way and to encourage you to continue to search for the full answers. Many of the statements in this chapter will be in the form of hypotheses—preliminary guesses at the truth. By using this style of approach, we can keep continually before us the idea that the field we are working in is an open, growing field.

Perhaps the most frequently heard "commonsense" strategy is: What we need is more education. Granted the enormous complexity of discrimination, this is a gross oversimplification. My first inclination is to argue against it or to point out its inadequacy. It may be valuable, however, to adopt a different approach. Let us agree on the great need for more education but equally agree that "education" shall be defined in very broad terms. Nothing else, in fact, seems adequate in the kind of society we live in. In simpler societies, the only school is the house and the field, where those who carry on the business of life train children by example and precept. But when societies become complex and subject to constant change, the parental model is incomplete; specialized teachers are required; the school is invented. Now we are moving to still a third stage where the school and college have become inadequate, at least insofar as we think of them as places where education is *completed*. Changes in the conditions of life are so extensive and rapid and perpetual that anything less than continuous education throughout a lifetime is inadequate.

It is easy for us to ask: How can a tribesman in the Congo train his son for what he will face in the years ahead? How can an Alabama sharecropper prepare his child for life on a Detroit assembly line? How can an illiterate peasant in Egypt provide his family with the skills and values demanded in the life of the city? It is more significant, however, for us to ask: How can a college-educated professional or business man, brought up in an era when oceans were wide and man's capacity for self-destruction had some spatial and temporal limits, teach his son and daughter the ways of the world? And how can a school or college, which releases its students twenty or thirty or forty years before they will make some of the central decisions of their lives, continue to be involved in their education? Only, of course, by implanting in them the intellectual modesty, the tentativity, the nagging curiosity that can keep them alert to the world of ideas and events throughout their lives.

This is the perspective of this chapter—a perspective that requires that one define education very broadly and refer to many events outside the classroom. It means that I shall raise many more questions than I shall answer, hoping to lay before you an exciting area for study and research, indicating possible paths, but making clear the need for much more knowledge. Some of you will furnish that knowledge.

Before turning to more specific problems of strategy, I must make one further preliminary observation: Neither education nor intergroup relations can be understood without reference to the society of which they are a part. The several institutions of a society, however much they may be studied separately, are best seen as part of an interacting system. Each part affects and is affected by the total system in which it is embedded. A person interested in understanding one aspect of society—religious patterns, for example— soon discovers that he cannot concentrate on explicitly religious groups and behavior alone. The constant interplay between religion and the economic, political, familial, and educational processes of society must be kept continually in mind.

The student of minority-majority relations faces the same reality. Wherever he may choose to begin his observations, he discovers that he is led, step by step, to the study of a complicated system of interlocking and mutually reenforcing patterns. There are, to be sure, contradictions and strains—weak points in the system that are subject to more rapid change. Both to the analyst and to the person trying to introduce change, these are strategically important facts; but they are best seen against the background of the way in which a society, despite its strains and inconsistencies, operates as one system. The person who seeks to understand, and to help others to understand, the roots of discrimination soon finds that the simple, commonsense formulas are in error primarily because they miss this interrelatedness of social life. "The basic problem is lack of job opportunities," or "You cannot legislate against prejudice," or "The fundamental issue is intermarriage"—such observations focus on one segment of life in such a way as to produce a distorted perspective.

There is another aspect to this view that intergroup relations are part of the "seamless web" of life. Strategies concerned only with social structure and strategies that give primary attention to individual attitudes furnish valuable but partial views of the forces involved in intergroup relations. Knowledge of the extent and depth of individual prejudice is an inadequate guide to knowledge of behavior. In a recent study of responses to a fair employment practices law, I found that union leaders expressed some individual prejudice, but supported without hesitation a strong antidiscriminatory policy. Management representatives, on the other hand, expressed less personal prejudice, but they tended to carry out discriminatory hiring practices. This does not mean that individual attitudes are unimportant; it means that they must be studied in the context of the group structure within which they are expressed. Oppositely, two persons who perform in similar roles and who are affected by similar situational influences may, nevertheless, respond differently because of differences in individual tendency. The student of intergroup relations cannot afford to disregard either the attitudes of individuals or the social structures within which they are expressed. He must explore the entire field.[1]

The complexity of the situation is well described by Deutsch and Collins on the basis of their study of integration in housing:

Our analysis of prejudice and discrimination suggests that any strategy of modifying race relations must have, at least, a fivefold objective: (a) a change in the political-economic relations in our society so that discrimination and prejudice come to fulfill no important purposes for socially influential groups . . . ; (b) a change in the objective socioeconomic status of Negroes [and other minorities] so that they may have full opportunity to participate in and contribute to the over-all American culture, so that they do not as a group bear the stigmata of discrimination and deprivation; (c) an elimination of the social practices of discrimination, exclusion, and segregation which serve to put Negroes at a social disadvantage and which act as a powerful reenforcement to prejudice;

(d) destruction of prejudiced attitudes which predispose the individual to discriminatory behavior and to the support of segregation; (e) the development of stronger allegiance to the democratic ideology.[2]

A one-variable approach is likely to be as ineffective as a quarter-back who knows only one play. This analogy may suggest that the *combination* of plays most likely to be successful depends upon the opposition, that is, upon the particular situation with which one is dealing. Our statement of general strategic principles of necessity disregards the problem of dealing with the balance of forces operating in specific settings. A further complexity to which we should be alert is that each of the issues described by Deutsch and Collins has its own internal structure. Chein has observed, for example, that individual prejudices (d, in the list above) have several dimensions associated with information (or lack thereof), conformity, status, and emotional need.[3] The kind of strategy that is effective in reducing one of these supports to prejudice may be quite ineffective in dealing with the others. The dimensions and related strategies might be charted as follows:

Dimension of prejudice	Approach likely to be effective
1. Lack of information, stereotyped view	1. Education, contact
2. Need to conform	2. Clear specification of legal and other standards of nondiscrimination
3. Desire for status; insecurity of status	3. Creating more secure life, more opportunity for all
4. Emotional need, feelings of hatred and hostility	4. Reduction of the frustrations of prejudiced persons

This is not a definitive list or a series of clearly separate analytic categories, but it can make us aware of the complexity of the supports for discrimination and of the need, therefore, for many different approaches. Note in particular that even in dealing with individual prejudice, most of the strategies suggested in the right-hand column above make no direct reference to individual attitudes. The aim, rather, is to create a situation in which stereotyped or hostile notions no longer have any function for the person. If you try to argue some-one out of his point of view, he is likely to argue back, to defend himself, to search for "good reasons" why he believes what he does. But if you change the circumstances of his life within which that point of view prospered and then offer him alternative ways of defin-ing the situation, his prejudice is much more likely to decline.

We shall use a concept of "education" of sufficient breadth to include the influences on learning that come from a change of cir-cumstance. If we accept the more common and literal meaning of the term, we will be liable to give excessive attention to individual atti-tudes and to neglect attention to the social situations within which these attitudes are expressed. It is easy to assume that if misconcep-tions can be reduced, if more knowledge can be brought to bear on the question, if authoritarian tendencies can be changed, then inter-group relations must certainly be affected. I would not want to dis-pute these propositions, as being partial truths, but would emphasize the need to see them in the context of other truths: Some persons will act in nondiscriminatory ways, despite their misconceptions or preju-dices, because the situation within which they behave facilitates the expression of different attitudes; they behave as union members or churchmen or businessmen or law-abiding citizens. Under many circumstances, to understand and to change behavior requires, not so much a direct attack—educational or otherwise—on prejudices, as an indirect attack. If one can change the reference group with which persons identify while viewing a problem or can change the balance of sanctions and rewards of the surrounding environment, he can often change their readiness for education and their behavior without direct attention to individual prejudices.

In some measure, attitudes, knowledge, and even lack of knowl-edge are functionally connected with one's group identity and with the whole complex of social forces at work in one's environment. Under these conditions, to attack lack of knowledge, for example, may be to attack a symptom. A person may be ignorant, not because of lack of opportunity to know the true state of affairs, but because of the great "convenience of ignorance," as Myrdal put it, in protecting and justifying one's actions. I talked recently with a famed lawyer and jurist, the dean of a law school, who was barely conversant with the most rudimentary facts concerning race relations in his region of the country. No need to talk about education in his case, so long as he was so deeply involved in a social structure and with groups that would find knowledge of the facts extremely inconvenient. Education is possible only in a supportive environment; and those who would promote intergroup education must be concerned with the whole system of social relationships within which education is carried on—relationships that can block or facilitate changes in knowledge, attitudes, and behavior.

This can be called the *principle of indirection*. At first glance it is a principle that leads to pessimism, because it holds that change cannot be produced simply by increasing the flow of information, by education in a narrow sense. But the principle has its optimistic side. It holds that the broad sweep of social forces may sustain and speed the educational process. Efforts that failed in one circumstance to improve intergroup relations by education may succeed in another situation where the developments in economics, community structure, or law give them support. This means that attention to the impact of the economic situation or to trends in housing, for example, is educational, in the deepest meaning of the term. It may help to create a situation in which, the convenience of ignorance having been reduced, more persons can "afford" to listen.

Put in another way, this means that it may be well to treat education as the dependent variable on occasion. From this point of view we do not ask, "Can we increase understanding and produce changes in behavior by direct educational efforts?" but, "Will changes in the law, or housing arrangements, or job situations make education possible?" Education then feeds back into the total situation as one of a series of causally interdependent variables.

Such a point of view makes life much more complicated; but if it is valid, we disregard it to our peril, for we carry on our efforts at understanding and change on the basis of overly simple assumptions. In this connection, ignorance is surely *inconvenient*, not convenient.

Some Principles of Democratic Education

Before examining various aspects of the strategy of education, I would like to mention several principles that will be taken for granted in the discussion. These principles, based on both psychological and sociological observations, are well known and well established, so that we need only point to them here, with a few qualifying statements:

1. Learning by a process in which one has taken an active part, both in the sense of helping to search out the facts and of feeling free to participate in discussion, is more likely to be followed by action consonant with the learning than is a process of passive reception of knowledge. This leads naturally to the belief that a wider circle of persons should be involved in the study of minority-majority relations as a social problem. The participation of many groups whose actions and values must change, to accomplish improvement in this field, is desirable. Changes in our society, some of which we shall discuss below, have made groups ready for intergroup education which might have been quite unresponsive even a few years ago. Efforts to bring them into the public debate are likely to be fruitful.

2. The values that underlie the educational situation, the rights, and the privileges of the participants affect what they learn and what they will do. If they are free to question, to complain, and even to denounce, they find it easier, at least under many conditions, to accept new ideas and patterns of behavior. In a nonauthoritarian and open setting with no ego threats, they feel less need to defend their old point of view or to rehearse it covertly.

3. The concept of the reference group is important for intergroup education.[4] The group one is participating in or carries in his imagination when he is making a judgment or acting affects that judgment or action. In terms of strategy, this concept raises a basic question: How is it possible to keep the classroom, the church discussion group, or the total community as the reference

group when an individual who is involved in intergroup activity returns to an occupational group, community, or family with different standards? It is perhaps at this point that the mass media are likely to be most effective. They can reaffirm democratic inclinations that have already been established by a more intensive experience. The media are not likely to be able to build those inclinations in the first place. (This statement is more a hypothesis than a tested principle.) More generally, reference-group theory suggests the need for a continuing follow-up of educational experience. A few lectures, a course in school, or one or two contacts with a group which is dedicated to changing attitudes and actions are unlikely to be effective if the individuals involved continuously have reference and membership groups pulling them in different directions.

4. Ethnocentrism—the belief that the values and norms of one's own group are better than those of others—is a natural product of naïve socialization. But self-conscious socialization to the idea that people differ in values, styles of life, religion, and race is also possible. Efforts to reduce hostility between groups clearly must promote the latter idea, but it does create a problem. Some critics of sociology and anthropology contend that efforts to reduce ethnocentrism lead only to an extreme relativism in which each individual becomes his own moral arbiter—a situation of moral anarchy. Since "the mores can make anything right," there are no firm grounds for choosing one value or action over another. Such extreme relativism is a possible, but in my judgment highly unlikely, result of efforts to promote tolerance and reduce ethnocentrism. It does not seem to be nearly so great a danger as the clashes promoted by intolerant and rigid absolutisms which, in view of their mutual contradictions, obviously cannot all be "absolute." Little can be contributed to the firmness of our moral foundation in this heterogeneous and changing world if each of us declares: Although my values and first premises are absolute, it is easy for me to see how relative are your own. For better or worse, thoughtful negotiation between groups with

different value systems is an inevitable part of modern life. If this makes it more difficult to accept the ultimate and changeless validity of one's own code of values, it does not remove the need for modest and sympathetic value choices, on the basis of consequences, among standards and practices of different relative merit. Moreover, the idea that none of us has been entirely successful in his efforts to imagine and to put into practice the highest and best for human life may in itself be a point of view that can help us to move in that direction.

Strategy Related to Social Stratification

Starting from the sociological point of view that efforts to reduce or solve a social problem, to be effective, must be contextual, we can explore various aspects of the social context in an effort to determine the ways in which they affect receptivity to change. One series of questions arises from current research in social stratification: To what degree do prejudice and the tendency to discriminate vary among social classes? Are any observed variations by class primarily a result of differences in attitudes, e.g., more "authoritarian personalities" in one group than another, or are they primarily a result of different social situations? What circumstances for various classes prohibit or encourage discriminatory acts, regardless of attitudes? Do variations in intergroup belief and practice rest primarily on subcultural differences, e.g., differences in the norms and values to which children are socialized in different classes, or are they more the product of variation in the satisfactions and strains which result from various locations in the social structure?

Such questions can be answered only inadequately at the present time. We have some knowledge of the vulnerability to intergroup hostility of various groups now caught in the strains of rapid structural change. The most vigorous opposition to desegregation in the South comes from areas of economic stagnation and declining population. Political movements that contain hostility toward other groups as a dominant theme are most likely to prosper among individuals whose occupations and ways of life are being seriously undermined by social change—among workers threatened by automation, for example, and among small businessmen who can see only difficulties ahead whether times are good or bad.[5]

It is precisely those who belong to groups that are under the most severe pressure, and therefore most likely to express intergroup hostility, who are least likely to be reached by any direct educational venture. Education that reaches only those who are willing to be educated *now* misses many strategically important persons. This point is illustrated by the story of the mayor of a small Italian town, who, weary of the failure of his people to become literate, decided to carry on an active campaign. He had the town plastered with signs: "Wait no longer! Learn to read!" The minister's message to the empty pew is equally ineffective. In Merton's terms, "the fallacy of group soliloquy" and "the fallacy of privatized solutions"—persons of democratic inclinations talking to each other and believing they have done something—are major risks. For this reason, those who are interested in reducing prejudice and discrimination must give some part of their effort to the task of helping to relocate into new places in the social structure those in the dominant group who are under severe pressure. Only when some of the most severe threats have been removed, when life holds some promise of dignity and security, will those who are now filled with bitterness and frustration be ready for change.

One of the most important aspects of the reduction of intergroup hostility by the reduction of strain is the development of hope. When the members of a group see *no* way out of their difficulties, when they feel utterly helpless, they are liable to accept symbolic schemes that promise them relief and a sense of meaning. They become "true believers." And their belief may be in the complete superiority of their race, religion, or nation. A preparatory task of the strategist must be to help to create alternative ways of struggling with their problems. By promoting an environment where their political voices can be heard, where job security can be found, where they have some say in their work situations, where they see improving opportunities for their children, one supports a situation within which they are ready for education—for the learning of new ideas about race relations.

These same principles apply to members of minority groups. Their own prejudices and hostilities are often deep-seated. To reach them with facts and accepted principles, to persuade them to accept democratic intergroup relations, requires the creation of a situation in which they see some hope. American Negroes, for example, are probably more authoritarian, on the average, and less supportive of civil liberties than are white persons. This situation will not be sharply improved simply by education defined as symbolic communication. It will be changed only by the development of an "educationally sensitive" situation for Negroes, that is, one where they find new ideas and attitudes meaningful because life holds more promise.

By these comments I do not mean to imply that prejudice and discrimination are primarily phenomena of disadvantaged persons. It is frequently the powerful and well-placed who defend a discriminatory situation. They may speak about minorities in politer terms; they may lament violence; but even as they do, their actions may strongly support the violence-creating practices. Minorities are often pawns in the internal power struggles of a society. Powerful individuals who profit from prejudice and discrimination do not easily learn the heavy costs society pays for prejudice and discrimination. Their education begins when their possibilities for gain are lowered —by wider voting rights, democratic labor unions, antidiscrimination laws, and the like.

The statement of a few hypotheses may help to focus our attention on the significance of social stratification in intergroup relations. Remember that these are not statements of fact, but *preliminary guesses at the truth,* designed to stimulate your thought on the question involved.

Intense or violent antiminority action often contains an element of deflected class antagonism. The vigorous opposition to the desegregation of Central High School, Little Rock, for example, may have been precipitated partly by the fact that the new, upper-class Hall High School was not being desegregated at the same time. I do not underestimate the difficulty of testing this hypothesis; but its statement may indicate the kind of relationship to which students of intergroup relations must be alert. If we pay attention only to attitudes, without seeing their relationship to the surrounding situation, our efforts to reduce the social problem will be largely wasted.

Intergroup prejudice and hostility are increased by social change that is undermining an established way of life without creating new and hopeful structures for the groups being affected. Specific hypotheses might be formed in connection with the Southern farmer, or the authoritarianism of the worker who is threatened by automation and economic insecurity, or the "status panic" and possible anti-Semitism of some white-collar workers and small merchants, or, historically, the racism and attitudes toward immigration that were held by many residents of New England, including many of the intelligentsia, during the period of the decline of the influence of their region and of their ethnic groups. Perhaps you can select one of these groups and search out the evidence regarding the relationship of their prejudices to their life conditions.

In societies where the lower class is highly class conscious, it will tend to lack vigorous antiminority prejudices, for there will be some sense of solidarity with minorities; and the prejudices it does have will tend to be directed toward middle- and upper-class "minorities," e.g., Jews. Oppositely, in situations where the lower class is relatively lacking in class consciousness, as in the United States, it will tend to hold more prejudices and to discriminate more than do the upper classes or than do the lower classes in a more closed society.

The specific hypotheses mentioned here may be unimportant, but the problem they represent requires the careful attention of anyone who seeks to design effective strategy to improve intergroup relations. Knowledge of the nature of the social stratification system and of its effects on the attitudes and behavior of persons in different strata is essential to effective work. The extent and nature of prejudice vary from stratum to stratum; the degree of readiness for educational programs of various kinds or for social change is different in one class from what it is in another; the kinds of influences that must be changed before educational work, in a narrow sense, can even make a start, are not the same for members of different classes; and the class perspective of educational leaders themselves may, if they lead to overly simple assumptions and to blind spots, prevent effective work.

Strategic Consideration of Minority-group Members

Undoubtedly most of the efforts to improve intergroup relations are directed toward majority-group members, in an effort to reduce their prejudices and their tendencies toward discrimination. Under conditions of severe disprivilege for one or more minorities, this is an appropriate emphasis. As the total situation improves, however, it is wise to shift more attention to the minority-group members whose responses to disprivilege, although in the first instance an *effect* of prejudice and discrimination, become part of the cycle of causation. In an earlier chapter we referred to the theory of the vicious circle or, more neutrally, the self-fulfilling prophecy. The evidences for the operation of such a cycle in intergroup relations are evident on every hand. One of the tragic aspects of this phenomenon is that there is a generation or more of lag in the responses of many minority-group members to their environment. The lack of ambition, responsibility, or lawfulness that can be seen as natural *results* of segregation and persecution may continue almost unabated for many years after there has been a substantial reduction in their cause. Such responses feed back into the causal system and prevent the system's being eliminated as rapidly as might otherwise occur.

I recently asked many persons in a Northern industrial community which of the following changes would contribute more to the full integration of Puerto Ricans and Negroes into the community: first, the elimination of every evidence of *present* prejudice and discrimination; second, the elimination of the lack of ambition, of the relative unwillingness of many minority-group persons to work hard to acquire a skill, and of other evidences of *past* discrimination. The great majority of my respondents, both colored and white, chose the latter as likely to bring the greater gain. I am not at all certain that they are correct, but the question can scarcely be answered by anything more than an informed guess in any event. And I do not have implicit in the question any "vocabulary of praise and blame." Whatever the facts, they are natural products of the existing situation. But the question does suggest an important issue: We may be getting to the point, in some communities at least, where the greater problem is not that of eliminating the biases and misconceptions of the majority, but of training minority-group members to seize the opportunities now open to them.

To work effectively on this problem will require the answering of many questions. Put generally, we may ask: Which conditions promote, which ones weaken minority subcultures and personality tendencies that prevent the entrance of minority-group members into the full range of community life? How are families and schools involved? What are the influences of segregated housing and churches? What kinds of leaders are brought to the fore, in disprivileged and powerful groups alike, under present conditions?

At first glance, it may seem almost absurd to suggest that there is much of a gap in the education of minority-group members with respect to their rights, opportunities, and responsibilities in contemporary America. In a society where there are hundreds of organizations devoted to the improvement of intergroup relations and to the extension of the rights of minorities, it is easy to imagine that the messages of these groups are diffused almost everywhere. The NAACP has been making headline news for years. The National Conference of Christians and Jews, working on both national and local levels, the Anti-Defamation League, the Alianza Hispano-Americana, the Japanese-American Defense League, the Urban League, the Congress of Racial Equality, the Student Nonviolent Coordinating Committee—to mention only a few of the organizations at work—illustrate the range of the private groups in this field. In addition there are scores of local and national public bodies whose assigned task is the promotion of harmonious intergroup relations in one way or another—primarily by efforts to equalize the opportunities of minority-group members.

In the face of all this it must still be said—although the evidence is not definitive—that many persons in disprivileged circumstances are relatively untouched by any of these organizations. The majority of the citizens of a state will know nothing about the existence of a fair employment practices law even several years after it has been put into operation. Or, knowing of the law, they discount its value on the basis of their past experiences. In the subtle shaping of the attitudes of one's children as well as in more formal advice, many parents reveal a deep-seated pessimism, if not cynicism, that helps to create some of the tendencies on the basis of which prejudiced persons continue to justify their attitudes and actions. As one Negro put it, when asked about advice he would give his son in view of a newly passed fair employment practices law, with which he was unfamiliar: "No need to git an education. You can't fight them big wheels." Some of the effects of such an attitude, conveyed to children in many ways through the years, are high drop-out rate from school, failure to enroll in technical programs that lead to higher job levels, and entrance into low-pay, low-prestige occupations that serve to reenforce the cycle in the next generation.

We should not forget, of course, that many members of disprivileged groups have seized the opportunities that are opening to them, have pressed against the barriers of discrimination, and have been reached by and have taken part in educational efforts to improve intergroup relations. Isolation from the forces of change has undoubtedly become much less prevalent. The scope of Negro participation in the civil rights movement of the 1960s, which we shall discuss in the next section, is much wider than that in any previous effort to eliminate patterns of discrimination. Nor should we forget that there are many real obstacles which indicate that, in some measure, negative attitudes are a sign not of cynicism but of realism. We need, however, to note that under some circumstances there is a substantial, and understandable, lag in the responses of many minority-group members. At this point those engaged in educational efforts, in the broadest meaning of the term, have one of their most important opportunities.

There are many unanswered questions connected with this problem: Who is ready for education; who has been so deeply affected by discrimination that other strategies must be used? What kinds of educational efforts will be most effective—work done directly with parents and family groups, with schools, with church groups, through the mass media? The answers to these questions will vary from one circumstance to another. What will be effective in one community, with one group, may not be in another.

Educational efforts among parents who are rural migrants, for example, may be relatively less effective than efforts within schools to reach the children directly, to change their aspirations and values. It takes time to learn to live in a city, to know its opportunities, to acquire the skills, habits, and values that city life requires. Rural-migrant parents may mistrain their children because they depend upon experience that was gained in a significantly different environment. In a sense the continuity of generations will, and has to be, broken, if not by planned educational work and community effort, then by social disorganization. We see this most clearly and poignantly in the Negro slums at the heart of most of our large cities. The inadequacies of parental experience are compounded by the high proportion of broken and unstable families—plus, of course, the heavy load of discrimination. Undoubtedly the children of rural migrants are vitally dependent upon the school, and other educational work, to learn the requirements and possibilities of life in an urban society. If this proposition is correct, our society's inadequate support of schools, particularly in those areas where they are most needed for this purpose, compounds the tragedies of undemocratic intergroup relations. In the second generation, family life has become somewhat more stable, there are a few models to help shape the aspirations of children, and a few minority-group churches have added to their messages of transcendental hope some attention to life around them—even though it is sometimes stridently racist attention. These improvements lend support to the other forces that are working to solve the social problems associated with minority status.

Not all rural-migrant groups are alike, however. They vary particularly in the strength of their family traditions, a fact which is important in selecting the kind of educational work that may be effective with them. In one community known to the author, for example, Puerto Rican families tend to be well unified and bound together in ethnic organizations. Intergroup education directed toward families in this situation is likely to be effective—not, to be sure, as a substitute for work in the schools and elsewhere—but as a supporting activity. Where family life is much more disorganized, a large share of the strategic efforts to break the cycle of discrimination will have to be directed through other channels.

The Civil Rights Movement

Beginning, we might say arbitrarily, with the founding of the National Association for the Advancement of Colored People, in 1908, but coming vividly to the attention of the general public only half a century later, the civil rights movement has increasingly become the dominant force in efforts to reduce discrimination in the United States. Although the civil rights movement still involves only a small proportion of Negroes, as I suggested in the preceding section, there can be no doubt that in the last few years it has drawn its supporters from an ever-widening circle. With this enlargement, and with the accomplishment of some of its goals, the aims of the movement have also been enlarged. Many of its earliest efforts were devoted to arguing strategic cases before the Supreme Court in an effort to get an interpretation of the United States Constitution favorable to the demands for equality. No such job is ever completed, of course, but it would not be far wrong to say that between 1915 and 1960 the constitutional setting for minority-majority relations was transformed from one permitting discrimination and segregation, even by public bodies, to one forbidding them wherever there was public involvement on any level.

Along with the campaign to get favorable court decisions, civil rights groups began to devise means for getting laws enforced and new laws passed that were designed to reduce or eliminate discrimination. There are now hundreds of Federal, state, and local laws which proscribe inequality of treatment in voting, job opportunities, housing, education, and the use of public accomodations. To get a law passed is not the same, of course, as getting it enforced, and we shall comment on this question of effectiveness below.

In recent years, the civil rights movement has enlarged its interests to include a more direct approach to merchants, employers, and school officials, in an effort to win or force their acceptance of equal opportunities. Sit-ins, boycotts, picket lines, and other vigorous methods have, particularly since 1960, become an important part of the strategy of those who seek to abolish racial discrimination. This movement has been dominated by an emphasis on nonviolence and on the acceptance of suffering if need be that derive both from Christian teachings and from Gandhi. Participants in the protest campaigns have not always lived up to this ideal, but self-disciplined and nonviolent demonstrations have by far been more common. This is particularly remarkable in view of the violence to which demonstrators have been subjected in many instances.

We cannot take time to describe the many manifestations of this civil rights movement.[6] In one six-month period in 1963, there were over a thousand demonstrations, sit-ins, boycotts, rallies, kneel-ins, wade-ins, and picket lines; they took place in every part of the country; hundreds of thousands of persons were involved. Rather than to describe these events, our task is to ask why they occurred and why they have mounted to such a crescendo, and to inquire about their effectiveness as strategy.

Many of the facts we cited in Chapter 5 give us an indication of why the civil rights movement developed. For twenty-five years Negroes had experienced rapid improvement in status and income—but about 1955 the progress began to stall. In 1954, their hopes were raised enormously by the Supreme Court decision requiring the desegregation of schools, but by the early 1960s it was painfully apparent that only a fraction of the task had been accomplished. It is important to note that "the Negro revolt" followed a period of rapid improvement. There is now a substantial Negro middle class; 200,000 or more young Negroes are in colleges and professional schools; millions are residents in cities, where they can see the opportunities for advancement all around them. As is nearly always true in a revolutionary movement, it is not those on the bottom, but those who have experienced significant gains and then been stalled, who revolt. In absolute terms, America's nonwhites are well-off; in relative terms, in the mid-1960s, they are aware of serious disadvantages: The improvements they have won in the last few years are smaller than gains of the white population; hence they are falling farther behind. The improvements have been less rapid than the increase in their hopes; hence they are falling behind there also. And the gains for Negroes have been significantly less than those for other racial minorities, some of whom are rapidly overcoming their disprivileged positions; hence Negroes are falling behind in relative terms in this regard also.

The result: persistent, explosive, dramatic protest. Has it been effective? Is this the way to help solve a social problem? In my judgment, yes. The civil rights movement is a necessary and valuable *part* of a balanced strategic plan. That does not mean, of course, that it can be effective as a sole strategy, that it does not entail losses, or that it will accomplish all of its goals. Its main functions, as I see them, are three: As a dramatic and controversial movement it has brought inescapably to public attention the plight and the demands of nonwhite Americans. Although many dominant-group members have been sympathetic with the problem for many years, they have been content with a very modest rate of improvement and have been insensitive to the depth of disprivilege and resentment. Negro Americans have for the last few years been saying in a very loud voice: We are not willing to project our hopes onto our great, great-grandchildren (who are about the first who might expect substantial equality of treatment if the rate of change of the 1940s and 1950s were to continue). Now the issue is unmistakably before us. It has taken this enormous shout of protest to overcome the deafness of most white men on this question. Virtually everybody is now aware of the problem and knows that it will not simply solve itself; it has indeed become a social problem.

A second major influence of the civil rights movement is that it has decisively changed the *public* definition of minority-majority relations. Individual and private prejudice and discrimination may have been little affected; but the steady stream of laws, court decisions, administrative rulings, and the like has created a legal, political, and judicial structure now largely designed to establish equality of treatment. Private prejudices have a much narrower field within which to operate. The pull of conformity—a powerful pull in most of us—is more and more in the direction of nondiscrimination. And a context has been created within which the quieter strategies of education, negotiation, and conciliation can work much more effectively.

Perhaps most importantly of all, the civil rights movement has had an enormous impact on Negroes. They are now acting, and not simply reacting to their situation.[7] For generations they have accommodated themselves, often with great skill, to exceedingly difficult conditions; now they are struggling with those conditions, for they have developed the educational, political, and economic strength to do it. Although I cannot demonstrate this with any degree of adequacy, it is my strong impression that Negro self-respect has increased greatly in the last few years. Negroes have taken a stand, have suffered for it, and have won notable victories. The whole nation will gain from this transformation, for the presence of a group essentially lacking in self-respect is a costly burden. Such a condition is associated with low motivation, slight sense of responsibility, unused skills, attacks upon oneself such as alcoholism and mental illness, and attacks upon the society. Most gains are associated with some loss, and it may be that the rise in self-respect and self-confidence among Negroes has some "rough edges"—some awkward and exaggerated forms of expression—but on balance, this development is a valuable and essential part of the effort to improve race relations.

As a strategy, the civil rights movement carries some risks. Pressure from a minority may activate counterpressure by the majority. There is no doubt that the attitudes and actions of some white persons have hardened in the last several years, as the economic pressures, the fight against Negro efforts to register for voting, the opposition to desegregation of schools, and the violence clearly indicate. These are largely Southern phenomena, but in the North there is some evidence that ethnic groups whose own majority status is insecure and some individuals who feel uncertain of their own position are beginning to feel more strongly that change is occurring too fast, that Negroes are demanding too much. This risk, however, is easy to exaggerate. The civil rights movement may have brought opposition into the open, but not increased it. It may be easier to deal with it in its open—and often harshly discriminatory —form than in the hidden and quiet form of an earlier period. Those who are ready to murder to prevent Negroes from achieving equality, to mention the most extreme situation, undoubtedly increase support for the Negro cause and thus accomplish the opposite of what they intend.

A risk more serious than the arousal of opposition faces the civil rights movement. So far, the movement has been dominated in a surprisingly effective way by a nonviolent ideology. As more and more persons are drawn in, however, and as wider goals are sought, this ideal becomes more difficult to maintain. One aspect of the movement is civil disobedience—explicit and knowing violation of a hated law. In almost every instance this is done by persons ready to accept, without resistance, the punishment that comes from law violation; for they believe that they can thus dramatize to the nation the injustice in many laws. Civil disobedience is nothing new to the United States, of course. In a sense, the nation was founded by an organized campaign of civil disobedience, led by our earliest national heroes. And many Americans have something of Henry David Thoreau in them. Purely as strategy, however, civil disobedience is likely to be useful to a minority group—a group that by definition is relatively lacking in power—only if it remains nonviolent.[8] Violence will certainly be met by superior counterviolence. It also undercuts the moral foundation of the demands for equal rights, because it represents a denial to others of the very rights being sought for oneself.

On balance, I would regard the civil rights movement as highly effective strategy. The dangers within it are least likely to develop if the growth toward equality is rapid. And insofar as it succeeds, it is likely to be complemented more and more, and to some degree supplanted, by other strategies, some of which we shall consider in the next chapter.

8

BEYOND LEGAL EQUALITY:

the contact hypothesis

One of the most widespread commonsense ideas about intergroup relations is the declaration that "if people only knew each other better," there would be less prejudice and hostility. Like many commonsense ideas, it contains a substantial truth, but because the proposition as stated makes no reference to the conditions under which it is true, it can lead to error as often as to understanding. The statement is based on several sociological and psychological assumptions: that stereotypes thrive on misinformation; that hostile feelings are often directed toward images of what the members of a group are presumed to be like, and tend to be abated in contact with specific persons; that joint participation in an activity of mutual interest and value leads to a reassignment of the outgroup member to a fellow activity-group member.

A little thought reveals, of course, that contact may lead to heightened hostility, not to its abatement, that knowing the other person well may be the source of stronger, not weaker, opposition. There is more than a little sentimentality connected with this whole idea. Some persons have liberal ideas in intergroup relations only because they do *not* know the other person well—do not know the full extent of the contrasts in patterns of life or the personality damage caused by discrimination. Among such persons, thousands of whom, I venture to guess, graduate from our colleges every year, full-bodied education can be quite disillusioning. There may be a tendency, in various efforts to bring people together, to select contact so carefully, in the name of democracy and fairness, that many persons become acquainted with only part of the facts. When they learn some of the more uncomfortable facts—the existence of deep-seated value conflicts among religious groups, for example, or the presence of a hostile contraculture in the slums—their capacity for friendly intergroup relations may be seriously impaired.

The first important modification of the "contact hypothesis" was the proposition that it is *equal-status* contact across group boundaries that is likely to lead to more friendly intergroup relations. When professional man meets professional man, soldier meets soldier, sportsman meets sportsman across religious, racial, or national lines, prejudice and hostility are reduced. In such contacts, it is not the separating lines, but the unifying interests, values, and roles that most strongly affect the nature of the interaction. There is undoubtedly a great deal of truth in this idea. Those interested in improving intergroup relations have made, and can profitably continue to make, extensive use of equal-status contact as a strategy. There are, however, a number of questions that require further study: Does contact among those of equally *deprived* status have the same effects as contact among those of equally privileged status? Are the effects on an "ego-alien" or anxious person the same as on a stable person? Under what conditions does equal-status contact allow a person to say: Yes, he's all right, but he's an exception—thus preserving the "rule," and when does it attack the rule itself? What are the strategically most effective areas of interest within which equal-status contact promotes harmonious intergroup relations: housing, jobs, civic affairs, religious activities? Research designed to answer such questions as these could contribute greatly to the effective use of equal-status contact.[1]

Having isolated equal-status contact as an effective experience, we need now to go beyond it. There is the danger that such contact will be somewhat contrived or artificial, that it will produce a partial view of the world, that it will leave untouched the problems of hostility involved in *un*equal-status contact, that it will obscure some of the hard facts of life in America. Here as elsewhere "a little learning is a dangerous thing." It used to be said: The only Negro he knows is the janitor; the only Jew he knows is the owner of the surplus store. Although this is still true for many, now, paradoxically, it must be said of some that the only Negro he knows is the doctor, the only Jew the Reform Rabbi. Persons who might be the leaders in the improvement of intergroup relations are thus insulated from the most difficult facts and are therefore in no position to struggle effectively with the problems they represent.

It seems to follow clearly from these observations that intergroup experience that informs its participants of the full range of facts, that makes possible both equal- and unequal-status contacts, will be most effective in the long run in promoting harmonious human associations across group lines. If you seek to participate effectively in the reduction of discrimination, you will need a tough-minded realism about all aspects of minority-majority relations, not a few polite encounters in a church group or college discussion session.

Developments in City Life and Housing

Many of the principles suggested in the preceding section are pertinent to the study of contemporary changes in our cities. It is of vital importance that we ask: What is happening to our cities and their metropolitan areas? What is the long-run significance of present trends for intergroup relations?

The basic facts of contemporary urban growth are well known and need only to be mentioned here. Most of our large central cities are declining in population. This is a result of the rapid movement of the white population out of the city, only partly compensated for by the influx of colored population. Within a generation, if present trends continue, several of our largest cities will have populations less than 50 percent white. Meanwhile the suburbs, most of them segregated along racial lines and to some degree along religious lines, grow at a rapid rate. By 1960, over 25 percent of the population of the country resided in the suburbs. Here is an area in which new patterns and problems of intergroup relations are developing at great speed, largely without plan or forethought, and to an important degree as a result of the profit decisions and personal values of real estate developers.

Any strategic program that fails to explore the full implications of these facts would be very incomplete. There is more than a little danger that suburban residents, living in a white, middle-class area, and reading a book or taking a course in intergroup relations, will come to think of the problems in terms of sit-ins in Nashville, Freedom Riders in Mississippi, or delinquent gangs in the downtown area, without realizing the extent to which their suburbs are fully implicated in the total system of human relationships that prevails. It is perhaps not impossible that some intergroup relations teachers and leaders will make the same error. I can remember addressing a workshop group in an almost lily-white suburb and remarking that problems close at home were of considerable interest. I rebuked them —gently, I thought—for the paper curtain they had built between themselves and the downtown area; but this was not the kind of topic that the superintendent of schools, the three or four school board members present, and many of the teachers in the workshop thought was appropriate to the study of intergroup relations.

Were they correct? Or is the examination of the total, long-run consequences of metropolitan patterns one of the central concerns? If the "social system" concept is valid, the latter is clearly true. There is no way of isolating the suburb from the total stream of national life. What goes on in the central city affects and is affected by the policies and practices of the surrounding area. Before the end of this decade, over half of the Negro population of the country will live in the North and the West. Unless dramatic changes occur, many of them will still be attending quasi-segregated schools and residing in over-crowded and deteriorated areas. There is little doubt that this is costly to society, although there is need for research to discover the extent and the precise kinds of cost. Let me indicate some of the directions in which explorations of this problem might go:

The present metropolitan structure contributes to the maintenance of separating subcultures and contracultures among racial and ethnic minorities, with consequent loss of skills, intergroup conflict, increased criminaliy, and the deterioration of the inner city. It would be too blunt and overly simple to say that the real estate man and suburban developer and their clients *cause* crime and conflict—many of their activities are carried on in the name of avoiding such problems. But I suggest as a preliminary guess at the truth that their actions are in the cycle of causation that has such consequences. The statements above are not intended to imply an "antipluralism" value—that is, opposition to the maintenance of distinctive value systems in American society. We have discussed pluralism in Chapter 6 and need to say here only that there are limits to the range of values and actions that a society can sustain. Subcultures that are the products, not of distinctive histories and traditions, but of frustration, the absence of hope, conflict, and the *lack* of a guiding tradition are acceptable to almost no one. I prefer to call such systems of practices and values *contracultures,* not subcultures, to emphasize their origin in a conflict-laden and deprived situation. Their values are "reaction-formations," inverted norms that express the resentment of an oppressed group whose members have caught the image of human dignity but are deprived of the means for achieving it in their own lives.

The same hypothesis can be stated positively: Metropolitan areas within which all residents are free to choose their locations on the basis of income, family needs, and interests, without being con-strained by race, religion, or national origin, are areas where divisive contracultures do not prosper, where the aspirations of minority-group members are raised, and where prejudices are reduced. The proposition can scarcely be tested in this broad form, but it would not be difficult to devise research projects of more limited scope that would contribute to its exploration. Such research, indeed, has been carried out with reference specifically to the influence of interracial housing on attitudes and actions, and gives support to this hypothesis:

Fully integrated housing reduces prejudices and promotes friendly interracial relations.[2] The need now is to produce more differentiated hypotheses that test the influence of different proportions of majority and minority groups, of variation in support by the surrounding community, of the presence or absence of legal norms regarding segregated housing, and of other factors. There is much in this area that we do not know. And unhappily, most of what is known is opposed by the commonsense formulas by which men often guide their behavior; therefore knowledge on this question is adopted very slowly.

Misinformation on the question of housing is based substantially on the tendency to apply "facts" from observations of slums or of racially changing neighborhoods to all interracial or mixed areas— Negroes and Puerto Ricans live in slums; therefore they make slums. Or: Persons of Mexican origin live in slums; therefore if they are permitted to move into my neighborhood, it will become a slum. Or, observing a situation where a minority group, after piling up in a constricted area, finally breaks the barriers and spreads rapidly into the surrounding areas: Once change begins, an area soon is taken over completely by the minority group; therefore I must resist any change. Or: if the dam breaks, I must sell and run. Each of these statements is based on observation of a sort; they are not entirely irrational. The difficulty is that they convert limited observations into general principles. The need is for differentiated analysis that will seek out the conditions under which various results occur. It is sometimes true that once a minority-group member moves onto a block, the block is rapidly taken over by his fellow group members. Why? What is the influence of housing shortage, of governmental policy, of the informal agreements among real estate men, of the lending policies of banking institutions? It is sometimes true that after Negroes move into an area it deteriorates. Why? Was it already on the decline before they moved in; were they able to move in only because it was deteriorating; does their low income prevent adequate care; does a segregated subculture fail to teach them the techniques and values of good housing; is there a rental overcharge that can be carried only by overcrowding? In no area are our simple common-sense notions so obviously inadequate to explain the full range of the facts.

Ten years ago there were few firm facts by means of which we could correct these notions. This was partly due to the lack of study and partly to the almost total absence of mixed housing, except for temporary mixtures during periods of racial change-over. Now both of these situations are changing. There are scores of interracial residential areas, both private and public, and they are being care-fully studied.[3] Even the nonspecialist needs no longer to base his beliefs solely on observations of the tension-laden "invasion" of formerly restricted areas by vastly overcrowded minorities. The beginnings of differentiated analysis are now possible and permit the statement of further hypotheses in this area. These are as follows:

In stable neighborhoods, the establishment of a "benign quota" (a range of 25 to 30 percent is often mentioned) for newcomers of a different race or ethnic group can help to preserve the intergroup nature of the area.[4] There is an important moral as well as a research problem in this statement. Many persons respond negatively to any thought of a quota, even if its aim is the preservation of an interracial neighborhood which they support. The moral question is particularly complicated if members of the minority group are seriously disadvantaged in the securing of housing in the surrounding area. Intergroup education can profitably explore the moral dilemma involved in this kind of situation.

Fair housing practices legislation can support the present small trend toward "open occupancy" in housing. Experience with such laws is at present too slight to permit extreme confidence that this proposition, when framed as a specific hypothesis and tested, will prove to be correct. Doubtless the longer experience with fair employment practices laws, however, furnishes valuable guidance.

We know that a law wins support from some people because it makes an act official and right, weakening the validity of contrary informal norms in their eyes. A law can have an educational effect by helping to focus attention on a problem that previously had been disregarded by most people. It can inhibit the action of those who fear its sanctions. And it can weaken the argument of those who say that they would make a given change were it not for the competitive disadvantage in which it would place them.

In this whole area of community development and housing, the strategist will do well to seek the attention of real estate firms, builders, and bankers, as well as the members of various groups who seek housing or are interested in changing the patterns of segregation. Gradual changes in the general climate of opinion in the last fifteen years, the slowly increasing experience with open-occupancy situations, and many careful studies of housing have created a setting in which education in this area is now at least a possibility. Even a few years ago, if a builder had asked, "What will happen to my investment if I open my project to all comers?" one might have answered him by a statement of faith or perhaps by reference to facts in a racially changing neighborhood, soon to be all-Negro or all-Puerto Rican. But today the prospects under various conditions can be spelled out with tentative adequacy, at least. This is one area in which a simple extension of knowledge of the true facts among strategically placed groups may affect behavior in a significant way.

Educating the Employer in Intergroup Relations

Many of the observations with respect to housing are applicable also to employment. Before the Second World War, one could appeal to democratic values in support of nondiscriminatory employment, but if someone said, "I'm a hardheaded businessman. Will my customers stay away if I hire a minority-group clerk?" or, "Can a Negro do this job; and will my other employees work beside him?" one often could not answer him with the kind of evidence he required. Today the situation is different. There has been sufficient change in the facts of employment and sufficient observation and analysis of those facts that we can answer such questions with some confidence. It seems unlikely that the education of employers has kept up with the possibilities for such education. With a few exceptions, there is greater likelihood that change will be initiated as a result of labor shortage, legal pressure, boycott, or union policy than as a result of employer judgment that change is to his benefit and of value to the community. Some of the forces mentioned may prevent change as well, of course. The facts of the employment situation are by no means simple and do not necessarily lead an employer quickly to the conclusion that he should draw no religious, ethnic, or racial lines in his hiring policy. There are some risks, particularly in the short run. The total society certainly stands to gain by fuller use of its human resources, and that is why many states have sought, by passing fair employment practices laws, to protect themselves against the risks of inadequate use of their workers. The employer shares in the social gains and in the long run serves his own interests by having a larger labor pool to draw from and by attracting new purchasers into his market.

Efforts to modify existing patterns of minority-majority relations in employment can now draw on a substantial body of facts, on the reports and interpretations of fair employment commissions, and on other scholarly studies.[5] Such propositions as the following now seem to be correct under most conditions:

1. Completely open hiring policies reduce labor costs.
2. In the North at least, white workers will accept Negro supervisors of demonstrated competence.
3. Minority-group clerks do not repel customers.
4. Negro employees of equivalent background and experience perform as well as white workers.

These are merely illustrative of propositions that deserve further study but which at the moment seem to be true. For the most part, they support the view that there are important gains associated with a completely open employment policy. Employer and worker participation in exploring these facts can help to show that fears associated with changes in employment practices are often unfounded. In such contexts, there can be some redefining of the reference group that is operative while one assesses the employment situation.

The Impact of the College and School on Intergroup Relations

What is the effect of education on prejudice and discrimination? I refer not to specific intergroup relations courses or materials but to the general impact of the school as part of the total social system. There can be little doubt that the economic, political, religious, familial, and neighborhood patterns that surround a school system strongly influence, although they do not wholly determine, whatever lessons in intergroup relations may be taught.[6] If the surrounding institutions support intolerance and antipathy, the school is unlikely to initiate programs designed to promote intergroup harmony. If, because of some unusual combination of circumstances, such programs are adopted, their effectiveness is drastically curtailed by the contrary educational influence of out-of-school observations and experiences. It is a mistake to think of the school as a mere creature of its environment, unable in any way to depart from the values and standards of its supporting community. But it is equally a mistake to assume that its work is carried on independently. Such autonomous influence as the school possesses is based on the fact that teachers and school officials often feel the pull of a reference group of educators and the larger society, whose standards are broader than the community reference group which also affects their work.

It is the opposite point, however, that I would like to emphasize, with reference again to the principle of indirection: Attention to the economic and housing arrangements of his community, for example, may be the first order of business for the school board member or other citizen, and for the teacher or administrator who wants to make his school an agency for democratic education. If these arrangements create job distributions that correspond to the stereotype, if they reenforce separating subcultures or promote minority contracultures, if they produce *de facto* school segregation, they create a situation that makes intergroup education within the school or college difficult if not impossible. Recently the vocational guidance officer of a large public high school said to me that he felt obliged to discourage Negro boys who sought to enroll in certain programs for skilled training. Their opportunities in the community were so few, he noted, that they were likely to be disillusioned and embittered. (I disagree with his judgment: It is partly lack of training that creates lack of opportunity, not only vice versa; there are more opportunities elsewhere that can be sought out in this mobile world; and patterns are changing so that boys have to be taught to think in terms of what will be true in a few years, not what is true today.) In his hands, the school reenforced, with good intentions perhaps, discriminatory practices. Vigorous work among employers and unions to secure the placement of Negro boys in vocational programs might well have more educational effect on white boys who worked with them—and on vocational guidance officers—than the most intensive formal study of intergroup relations.

The way in which the school is tied to the community can also be illustrated positively: When, as a result of the development of intergroup housing, court order, or school board policy in the districting of a community, schools are desegregated, many forces are set in motion that directly and indirectly affect intergroup relations. A series of questions that can suggest the nature of the influence: Under what conditions is hostility among the students reduced or increased? How is the total value system of the school affected (its attention to academic training, athletics, social climbing, and other interests)? What are the influences on the aspirations of the members of various groups? Are the attitudes of and toward teachers affected? Are stereotypes changed? Do members of the formerly segregated groups take over the values and actions of the majority group, or are separate subcultures maintained?

Tested information on these questions is very scarce. The need is for longitudinal study that observes, under conditions as well controlled as possible, the consequences of different patterns. The hypotheses that I suggest here have a little evidence behind them, but require extensive research.

When a school is integrated, hostility between the formerly segregated groups of children occurs only if influential persons outside and inside the school, by their words and actions, condone and justify hostility. During the spring of 1958, Gertrude Samuels reported that the Little Rock high school was virtually governed by a group of fifty to a hundred die-hard segregationist students who were able to intimidate not only the eight Negro children, but most of the white students and the school administration. Though the facts were well-known, the city government did nothing, the school board felt helpless, and the state government furnished the moral ground on which the violent group stood. To state this in terms of the field view, the hostility was not *in* the students, but it was one potentiality, among many, which was made manifest by the particular influences at work in that setting.[7]

Over the years, but not all at once, an integrated school will help to eliminate the separating subcultures of disprivileged groups, thus destroying some of the facts that are used to justify intergroup hostility and discrimination. If this proposition is correct, the sheer fact of integration of schools has an important strategic impact. The point is of significance, not only to the South or to the Northern cities containing large minority areas, but to many small Northern communities as well. If there are three elementary schools in a town, one containing a large number—perhaps a majority—of Negroes, for example, while the other two have few or no Negroes, separating values may be maintained. By use of the Princeton Plan, which we described earlier, however, the problem can be reduced; and an opportunity for flexible and imaginative academic programs is simultaneously created.

A closely related proposition focuses on the individual and not the subcultural norms: An integrated school raises the aspirations and changes the behavior of formerly segregated children. There is a need to test this statement under varying circumstances. The proportionate sizes of various groups, the degree of preparation of teachers for the new arrangement, the extent to which the school gets strong community support, or fails to get support as many people move to the suburbs—these are among the variables involved.

Conclusion

I have attempted to suggest in this chapter and the previous one the kind of resource available from contemporary sociology to the person who is interested in the reduction of discrimination. The current level of knowledge on most of the questions that we have raised requires that one speak with caution. But the gains of recent years give confidence that the perspective of the student of society can contribute a great deal both to analysis and to the development of effective strategies. The increasing richness of the material on employment patterns, housing, social stratification, education, religion, and other areas vital to intergroup relations, challenges everyone concerned with this topic to reappraise continually both his factual knowledge and his presuppositions. Despite the headlines of conflict and difficulty, major social forces are promoting the growth of more democratic intergroup relations. This process, however, is not the result simply of impersonal social forces. It has developed and will be maintained by the actions of persons who know the trends and work to guide and accelerate them.

FOOTNOTES

Chapter One: The Study of Societies and Social Problems

1. Robert Merton takes a somewhat different position on this question in Robert Merton and Robert Nisbet (eds.), *Contemporary Social Problems,* Harcourt, Brace & World, Inc., New York, 1961, pp. 704–705.
2. This is a term associated particularly with an approach to social problems developed in Richard C. Fuller, "Sociological Theory and Social Problems," *Social Forces,* May, 1937, pp. 496–502; and in Richard C. Fuller and Richard R. Myers, "Some Aspects of a Theory of Social Problems," *American Sociological Review,* February, 1941, pp. 24–32.
3. Merton, *op. cit.,* p. 701.

Chapter Two: Social Stratification

1. See Max Weber, in Hans Gerth and C. Wright Mills (eds.), *From Max Weber,* Oxford University Press, Fair Lawn, N.J. 1946, pp. 180–195.
2. See Gerhard Lenski, "Status Crystallization: A Non-Vertical Dimension of Social Status," *American Sociological Review,* August, 1954, pp. 405–413; and Elton F. Jackson, "Status Consistency and Symptoms of Stress," *American Sociological Review,* August, 1962, pp. 469–480.
3. Kingsley Davis and Wilbert Moore, "Some Principles of Stratification," *American Sociological Review,* April, 1945, p. 243.
4. Dennis H. Wrong, "Functional Theory of Stratification," *American Sociological Review,* December, 1959, p. 774.
5. Walter Buckley, "Social Stratification and the Functional Theory of Social Differentiation," *American Sociological Review,* August, 1958, pp. 369–375.
6. See Seymour Martin Lipset and Reinhard Bendix, *Social Mobility in Industrial Societies,* University of California Press, Berkeley, Calif., 1959, p. 25.
7. See, e.g., Adrian C. Mayer, *Caste and Kinship in Central India,* University of California Press, Berkeley, Calif., 1960; J. H. Hutton, *Caste in India: Its Nature, Function, and Origins,* 3d ed., Oxford University Press, Fair Lawn, N.J., 1961; E. R. Leach (ed.), *Aspects of Caste in South India, Ceylon and North-west Pakistan,* Columbia University Press, New York, 1960.

8. Of the large literature on this subject, see Morris Rosenberg, "Perceptual Obstacles to Class Consciousness," *Social Forces*, October, 1953, pp. 22–27; Robin M. Williams, Jr., *American Society*, 2d ed., Alfred A. Knopf, Inc., New York, 1960, chap. 5; Gideon Sjoberg, "Are Social Classes in America Becoming More Rigid?" *American Sociological Review*, December, 1951, pp. 775–783; W. Lloyd Warner and James C. Abegglen, *Occupational Mobility in American Business and Industry, 1928–1952*, The University of Minnesota Press, Minneapolis, 1955; C. Wright Mills, *The Power Elite*, Oxford University Press, Fair Lawn, N.J., 1956; Ralf Dahrendorf, *Class and Class Conflict in Industrial Society*, Stanford University Press, Stanford, Calif., 1959; Milton M. Gordon, *Social Class in American Sociology*, The Duke University Press, Durham, N.C., 1958; Joseph Kahl, *American Class Structure*, Holt, Rinehart and Winston, Inc., New York, 1957; Leonard Riessman, *Class in American Society*, The Free Press of Glencoe, New York, 1960; and Bernard Barber, *Social Stratification*, Harcourt, Brace & World, Inc., New York, 1957.
9. Lipset and Bendix, *op. cit.*, p. 263.

Chapter Three: Minority Groups, Castes, and Classes

1. Louis Wirth in Ralph Linton (ed.), *The Science of Man in the World Crisis*, Columbia University Press, New York, 1945, p. 347.
2. See Frank Westie, "Negro-White Status Differentials and Social Distance," *American Sociological Review*, October, 1952, pp. 550–558, for a somewhat different formulation of this question.
3. See Benjamin Epstein and Arnold Forster, *Some of My Best Friends*, Farrar, Straus & Cudahy, Inc., New York, 1962, pp. 105–115.
4. These three criteria are used by Marvin Harris, "Caste, Class, and Minority," *Social Forces*, March, 1959, pp. 248–254.
5. See Gerald D. Berreman, "Caste in India and the United States," *American Journal of Sociology*, September, 1960, pp. 120–127.
6. For an excellent discussion of this question, see Charles Wagley and Marvin Harris, *Minorities in the New World*, Columbia University Press, New York, 1958.
7. See, e.g., Geoffrey Wheeler, *Racial Problems in Soviet Muslim Asia*, 2d ed., Oxford University Press, Fair Lawn, N.J., 1962; Walter J. Kolarz, "Race Relations in the Soviet Union," in Andrew W. Lind (ed.), *Race Relations in World Perspective*, University of Hawaii Press, Honolulu, 1954, chap. 9; and Moshe Decter, "The

Status of Jews in the Soviet Union," *Foreign Affairs*, January, 1963, pp. 420–430.

8. See S. N. Eisenstadt, *The Absorption of Immigrants*, Routledge & Kegan Paul, Ltd., London, 1954; and Judith Shuval, "Emerging Patterns of Ethnic Strain in Israel," *Social Forces*, May, 1962, pp. 323–330.

9. Dorothy Glass, *London's Newcomers*, Harvard University Press, Cambridge, Mass., 1961; J. A. G. Griffith et al., *Coloured Immigrants in Britain*, Oxford University Press, for the Institute of Race Relations, London, 1960; Michael Banton, *White and Coloured*, Rutgers University Press, New Brunswick, N.J., 1960.

10. See Norman Phillips, *The Tragedy of Apartheid*, David McKay Company, Inc., New York, 1961; Gwendolen Carter, *The Politics of Inequality. South Africa since 1948*, Thames and Hudson, Ltd., London, 1958; Hilda Kuper, *Indian People in Natal*, University of Natal Press, Pieter-Maritzburg, South Africa, 1960.

11. In Linton, *op. cit.*, pp. 347–372. Note, however, Wirth uses the term "militancy" for domination, though the latter term seems more useful, since other types of minorities may be militant.

12. On the Black Muslims, see C. Eric Lincoln, *The Black Muslims in America*, Beacon Press, Boston, 1961; and E. U. Essien-Udom, *Black Nationalism. A Search for Identity in America*, The University of Chicago Press, Chicago, 1962. For valuable recent discussions of pluralism and assimilation, see Nathan Glazer and Daniel P. Moynihan, *Beyond the Melting Pot: The Negroes, Puerto Ricans, Jews, Italians and Irish of New York City*, The M.I.T. Press and Harvard University Press, Cambridge, Mass., 1963; Milton M. Gordon, *Assimilation in American Life*, Oxford University Press, Fair Lawn, N.J., 1964; and Robin M. Williams, Jr., *Strangers Next Door*, Prentice-Hall, Inc., Englewood Cliffs, N.J., 1964.

13. Richard Schermerhorn, "Minorities: European and American," *Phylon*, Summer, 1959, p. 179.

14. *Yearbook on Human Rights for 1950*, United Nations, Department of Public Information, New York, 1952, p. 490.

15. Everett C. Hughes, "Race Relations in the Sociological Imagination," *American Sociological Review*, December, 1963, p. 883.

16. There is a very large body of literature dealing with the "personality" approach to prejudice and discrimination. A basic document is T. W. Adorno et al., *The Authoritarian Personality*, Harper & Row, Publishers, Incorporated, New York, 1950. The thesis of this book, however, requires careful qualification. See Richard Christie and Marie Jahoda (eds.), *Studies in the Scope and Method of "The*

Authoritarian Personality," The Free Press of Glencoe, New York, 1954; Richard Christie and Peggy Cook, "A Guide to Published Literature Relating to the Authoritarian Personality Through 1956," *Journal of Psychology,* April, 1959, pp. 171–199; Milton Rokeach, *The Open and Closed Mind,* Basic Books, Inc., Publishers, New York, 1960; and George E. Simpson and J. Milton Yinger, *Racial and Cultural Minorities,* 3d ed., Harper & Row, Publishers, Incorporated, New York, 1965.

17. On the concept of the self-fulfilling prophecy, see Gunnar Myrdal, *An American Dilemma,* Harper & Row, Publishers, Incorporated, New York, 1944, pp. 75–78; R. M. MacIver, *The More Perfect Union,* The Macmillan Company, New York, 1948, pp. 52–81; and Robert K. Merton, *Social Theory and Social Structure,* rev. ed., The Free Press of Glencoe, New York, 1957, pp. 421–436.

Chapter Four: Negroes in the United States

1. See Leo Kuper, "The Control of Social Change: A South African Experiment," *Social Forces,* October, 1954, pp. 19–29.
2. *The Wall Street Journal,* May 26, 1961, p. 1.
3. J. Milton Yinger and George E. Simpson, "Can Segregation Survive in an Industrial Society?" *Antioch Review,* Spring, 1958, pp. 16–17.
4. *Ibid.,* p. 17.
5. *The New York Times,* Sept. 9, 1963, p. E1.
6. *Report of the United States Commission on Civil Rights, 1961,* vol. 1, *Voting,* Government Printing Office, Washington, 1962.
7. *The New York Times,* Nov. 3, 1963, p. 69.
8. See Warren Breed, "Group Structure and Resistance to Desegregation in the Deep South," *Social Problems,* Summer, 1962, pp. 84–94; Thomas F. Pettigrew and Richard M. Cramer, "The Demography of Desegregation," *Journal of Social Issues,* 1959, vol. 15, no. 4, pp. 61–71; and Melvin M. Tumin, *Desegregation, Resistance and Readiness,* Princeton University Press, Princeton, N.J., 1958.
9. Ernest Q. Campbell, "On Desegregation and Matters Sociological," *Phylon,* Summer, 1961, pp. 135–145.

Chapter Five: Desegregation

1. James Baldwin, *The Fire Next Time,* The Dial Press, Inc., New York, 1963, p. 68.
2. *Report of the United States Commission on Civil Rights, 1963,* Government Printing Office, Washington, 1963, p. 218. See pp. 169–224 for their full discussion of integration in the Armed Forces.

3. United States Department of Labor, "The Economic Situation of Negroes in the United States," Bulletin S-3, revised, 1962.
4. The Hallmark Employment Agency in New York City, which specializes in the placement of Negroes in white-collar jobs, reported that placements in the first two months of 1964 were 50 percent higher than for the same period in 1963. See *Newsweek,* Mar. 23, 1964, pp. 86–88.
5. Commission on Race and Housing, *Where Shall We Live,* University of California Press, Berkeley, Calif., 1958.
6. See *ibid.* and Davis McEntire, *Residence and Race,* University of California Press, Berkeley, Calif., 1960.
7. See Eunice Grier and George Grier, *Privately Developed Interracial Housing: An Analysis of Experience,* University of California Press, Berkeley, Calif., 1960.
8. *Southern School News,* September, 1964, pp. 1 and 11; and Southern Education Reporting Service, *Statistical Summary,* 1963–1964, p. 2.
9. *Ibid.,* p. 3.
10. *Report of the United States Commission on Civil Rights, 1961,* vol. 2, *Education,* Government Printing Office, Washington, p. 174.
11. *Cleveland Press,* June 22, 1963, p. 9.
12. See Ernest Q. Campbell and Thomas F. Pettigrew, *Christianity in Racial Crisis. A Study of Little Rock's Ministry,* Public Affairs Press, Washington, 1959.
13. *The New York Times,* June 30, 1963, p. E8.
14. See Mathew Ahmann (ed.), *Race: Challenge to Religion,* Henry Regnery Company, Chicago, 1963; and Kyle Haselden, *The Racial Problem in Christian Perspective,* Harper & Row, Publishers, Incorporated, 1959.

Chapter Six: Goals in Intergroup Relations

1. Wayne A. R. Leys, in Joseph Gittler (ed.), *Understanding Minority Groups,* John Wiley & Sons, Inc., New York, 1956, p. 2. The whole statement by Leys, chap. 1 of this volume, is worth your study.
2. *Ibid.,* p. 9.
3. *Ibid.,* p. 13.
4. Data from State of Hawaii, Department of Planning and Research, furnished to me through the courtesy of Professor Douglas Yamamura.
5. For other discussions of these questions, see Oscar Handlin, issue editor, "Ethnic Groups in American Life," *Daedalus,* Spring, 1961; and Milton M. Gordon, *Assimilation in American Life,* Oxford University Press, Fair Lawn, N.J., 1964.

6. See J. Milton Yinger, "Contraculture and Subculture," *American Sociological Review,* October, 1960, pp. 625–635.

7. C. Eric Lincoln, *The Black Muslims in America,* Beacon Press, Boston, 1961; E. U. Essien-Udom, *Black Nationalism: A Search for Identity in America,* The University of Chicago Press, Chicago, 1962.

8. Lincoln, *op. cit.,* p. 17.

9. See J. Milton Yinger, *Sociology Looks at Religion,* The Macmillan Company, New York, 1963, pp. 104–111.

Chapter Seven: The Reduction of Discrimination

1. See George E. Simpson and J. Milton Yinger, *Racial and Cultural Minorities,* 3d ed., Harper & Row, Publishers, Incorporated, New York, 1965.

2. Morton Deutsch and Mary E. Collins, *Interracial Housing,* The University of Minnesota Press, Minneapolis, 1951, pp. 144–145.

3. Isidor Chein, "Some Considerations in Combating Intergroup Prejudice," *Journal of Educational Sociology,* March, 1946, pp. 412–419.

4. See Robert K. Merton, *Social Theory and Social Structure,* rev. ed., The Free Press of Glencoe, New York, 1957, chaps. 8 and 9.

5. There is an extensive literature on this subject. See, e.g., S. M. Lipset, "Democracy and Working-class Authoritarianism," *American Sociological Review,* August, 1959, pp. 482–501; Martin Trow, "Small Businessmen, Political Tolerance, and Support for McCarthy," *American Journal of Sociology,* November, 1958, pp. 270–281; Albert K. Cohen and Harold M. Hodges, "Characteristics of the Lower-blue-collar-class," *Social Problems,* Spring, 1963, pp. 303–334; Thomas F. Pettigrew, "Regional Differences in Anti-Negro Prejudice," *Journal of Abnormal and Social Psychology,* July, 1959, pp. 28–36; Fred B. Silberstein and Melvin Seeman, "Social Mobility and Prejudice," *American Journal of Sociology,* November, 1959, pp. 258–264; Frank R. Westie and Margaret L. Westie, "The Social Distance Pyramid: Relationships between Caste and Class," *American Journal of Sociology,* September, 1957, pp. 190–196.

6. See Martin Luther King, Jr., *Stride toward Freedom,* Harper & Row, Publishers, Incorporated, New York, 1958, and *Strength to Love,* Harper & Row, Publishers, Incorporated, New York, 1963; Louis E. Lomax, *The Negro Revolt,* Harper & Row, Publishers, Incorporated, New York, 1962; Merrill Proudfoot, *Diary of a Sit-in,* The University of North Carolina Press, Chapel Hill, N.C., 1962; James Peck, *Freedom Ride,* Simon and Schuster, Inc., New York, 1962.

7. Harold W. Pfautz, "The New 'New Negro': Emerging American," *Phylon*, Winter, 1963, pp. 360–368.

8. James W. Vander Zanden, "The Non-violent Resistance Movement against Segregation," *American Journal of Sociology*, March, 1963, pp. 544–550.

Chapter Eight: Beyond Legal Equality

1. For excellent materials on this question, see Muzafer Sherif et al., *Intergroup Conflict and Cooperation: The Robbers Cave Experiment*, The University Book Exchange, University of Oklahoma Press, Norman, Okla., 1961; Marian Radke Yarrow, issue editor, "Interpersonal Dynamics in a Desegregation Process," *Journal of Social Issues*, vol. 14, 1958; Robert Coles, *The Desegregation of Southern Schools: A Psychiatric Study*, Anti-Defamation League of B'nai B'rith and Southern Regional Council, New York, July, 1963.

2. See Morton Deutsch and Mary E, Collins, *Interracial Housing*, The University of Minnesota Press, Minneapolis, 1951; Daniel M. Wilner, Rosabelle P. Walkley, and Stuart K. Cook, *Human Relations in Interracial Housing*, The University of Minnesota Press, Minneapolis, 1955.

3. See, e.g., Nathan Glazer and Davis McEntire, *Studies in Housing and Minority Groups*, University of California Press, Berkeley, Calif., 1960; Eunice Grier and George Grier, *Privately Developed Interracial Housing*, University of California Press, Berkeley, Calif., 1960.

4. Oscar Cohen, "The Case for Benign Quotas in Housing," *Phylon*, Spring, 1960, pp. 20–29; Dan W. Dodson, "Can Intergroup Quotas Be Benign?," *Journal of Intergroup Relations*, Autumn, 1960, pp. 12–17.

5. See Jack Greenberg, *Race Relations and American Law*, Columbia University Press, New York, 1959, especially chap. 6; Paul H. Norgren et al., *Employing the Negro in American Industry*, Industrial Relations Counselors, Inc., New York, 1959.

6. Charles H. Stember, *Education and Attitude Change: The Effect of Schooling on Prejudice against Minority Groups*, Institute of Human Relations Press, New York, 1961.

7. For many useful comparative facts, see Coles, *op. cit.*